Introduction to *Daily Paragraph Editing*

Why *Daily Paragraph Editing?*

Daily Paragraph Editing is designed to help students master and retain grade-level skills in language mechanics and expression through focused, daily practice. Instead of practicing skills in a series of random, decontextualized exercises, *Daily Paragraph Editing* embeds language skills in paragraphs that represent the types of text that students encounter in their daily reading and writing activities across the curriculum. A weekly writing activity allows students to apply the skills they have been practicing throughout the week in their own short compositions.

What's in *Daily Paragraph Editing?*

Daily Paragraph Editing contains lessons for 36 weeks, with a separate lesson for each day.

Each week's lessons for Monday through Thursday consist of individual reproducible paragraphs that contain errors in the following skills:

- capitalization
- punctuation
- spelling
- language usage, and more

Student's daily lesson pages for Monday through Thursday include:

- a label indicating the type of writing modeled in the weekly lesson

- a paragraph with errors for students to correct; along with the other 3 paragraphs for the week, this forms a complete composition

- daily and weekly lesson identifiers

- as needed, the "Watch For" logo alerts students to more challenging skills to address in the paragraph

BOOK REVIEW: *Dinotopia*   **Daily Paragraph Editing**

Name _____

Dinotopia

where can you reed about humans and intelligent dinosaurs that have lived together for centuries? You can in james Gurney's series of books about a land of intelligent dinosaurs the first book in the series, <u>Dinotopia: A Land Apart from Time</u> introduces readers to biologist and explorer Arthur denison and his son will who are shipwrecked on a hidden island. there they encounter intelligent dinosaurs living in harmonee with marooned travelers

WATCH FOR
- spelling

MONDAY   **WEEK 28**

Students correct the errors in each daily paragraph by marking directly on the page. A reproducible sheet of Proofreading Marks (see page 10) helps familiarize students with the standard form for marking corrections on written text. Full-page Editing Keys show corrections for all errors in the daily paragraphs. Error Summaries help teachers identify the targeted skills in each week's lessons, and therefore help teachers plan to review or introduce the specific skills needed by their students.

Teacher's full-sized annotated Editing Key pages include:

• a label indicating the type of writing modeled in the weekly lesson

• the original student text with corrections marked in red (using the proofreading marks presented on page 10)

• daily and weekly lesson identifiers

• a summary of the errors in each paragraph to use in identifying unfamiliar skills to teach or review with students prior to assigning the paragraph. Some students may be more successful if you share the Error Summary with them before they read and edit the paragraph.

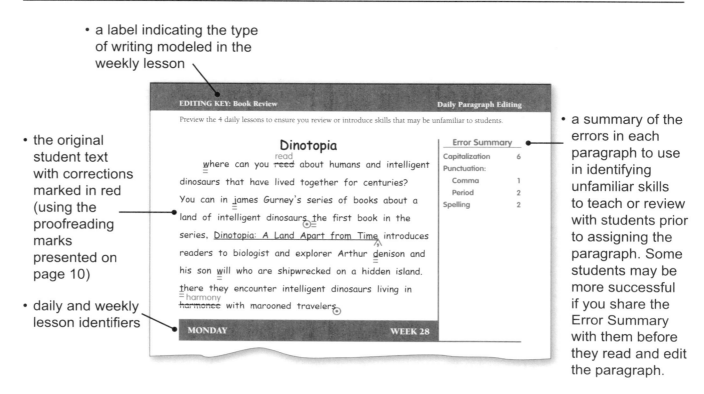

When corrected and read together, the four paragraphs for one week's lesson form a cohesive composition that also serves as a writing model for students. The weekly four-paragraph compositions cover a broad range of expository and narrative writing forms from across the curriculum, including the following:

• nonfiction texts on grade-level topics in social studies and science
• biographies, book reviews, editorials, instructions, interviews, journal entries, and letters
• fables, fantasy and science fiction, historical fiction, personal narratives, and realistic fiction

EMC 2728 • Daily Paragraph Editing • ©2004 by Evan-Moor Corp.

Each Friday lesson consists of a writing prompt that directs students to write in response to the week's four-paragraph composition. This gives students the opportunity to apply the skills they have practiced during the week in their own writing. Students gain experience writing in a wide variety of forms, always with the support of familiar models.

Friday writing prompts include:

• a prompt to write a composition in the same form as modeled in the weekly lesson

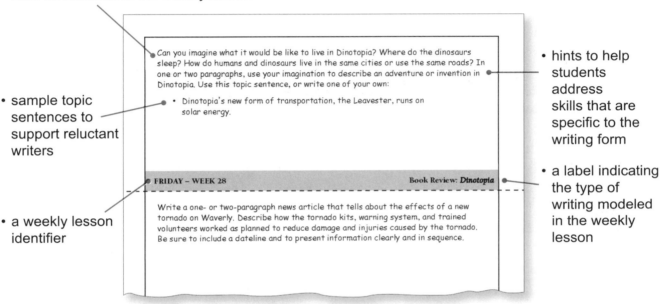

• sample topic sentences to support reluctant writers

• a weekly lesson identifier

Can you imagine what it would be like to live in Dinotopia? Where do the dinosaurs sleep? How do humans and dinosaurs live in the same cities or use the same roads? In one or two paragraphs, use your imagination to describe an adventure or invention in Dinotopia. Use this topic sentence, or write one of your own:

• Dinotopia's new form of transportation, the Leavester, runs on solar energy.

FRIDAY – WEEK 28   Book Review: *Dinotopia*

Write a one- or two-paragraph news article that tells about the effects of a new tornado on Waverly. Describe how the tornado kits, warning system, and trained volunteers worked as planned to reduce damage and injuries caused by the tornado. Be sure to include a dateline and to present information clearly and in sequence.

• hints to help students address skills that are specific to the writing form

• a label indicating the type of writing modeled in the weekly lesson

An Editing Checklist for students (see page 11) helps them revise their own writing or critique their peers' efforts. An Assessment Rubric (see page 9) is provided to help you assess student writing.

A reproducible student Language Handbook (pages 168–176) outlines the usage and mechanics rules for students to follow in editing the daily paragraphs. The Handbook includes examples to help familiarize students with how the conventions of language and mechanics are applied in authentic writing.

How to Use *Daily Paragraph Editing*

You may use *Daily Paragraph Editing* in several ways, depending on your instructional objectives and your students' needs. Over time, you will probably want to introduce each of the presentation strategies outlined below so you can identify the approach that works best for you and your students.

The four paragraphs that comprise each week's editing lessons include a set of errors that are repeated throughout all four paragraphs. We recommend that you provide a folder for students to keep their *Daily Paragraph Editing* reference materials and weekly lessons. It will work best to reproduce and distribute all four daily paragraphs for a given week on Monday. That way, students can use the previous days' lessons for reference as the week progresses.

Directed Group Lessons

Daily Paragraph Editing activities will be most successful if you first introduce them as a group activity. You might also have students edit individual copies of the day's lesson as you work through the paragraph with the group. Continue presenting the Monday through Thursday lessons to the entire class until you are confident that students are familiar with the editing process. Try any of the following methods to direct group lessons:

Option 1

1. Create and display an overhead transparency of the day's paragraph.

2. Read the paragraph aloud just as it is written, including all the errors.

3. Read the paragraph a second time, using phrasing and intonation that would be appropriate if all end punctuation were correct. (You may find it helpful to read from the Editing Key.) Read all other errors as they appear in the text.

4. Guide students in correcting all end punctuation and initial capitals in the paragraph; mark corrections in erasable pen on the overhead transparency.

5. After the paragraph is correctly divided into sentences, review it one sentence at a time. Have volunteers point out errors as you come to them, and identify the necessary corrections. Encourage students to explain the reason for each correction; explain or clarify any rules that are unfamiliar.

Option 2

Follow Steps 1–4 on page 4, and then work with students to focus on one type of error at a time, correcting all errors of the same type (i.e., capitalization, commas, subject/verb agreement, spelling, etc.) in the paragraph before moving on to another type. Refer to the Error Summary in the Editing Key to help you identify the various types of errors.

Option 3

Use directed group lesson time to conduct a minilesson on one or more of the skills emphasized in that day's lesson. This is especially appropriate for new or unfamiliar skills, or for skills that are especially challenging or confusing for students. After introducing a specific skill, use the approach outlined in Option 2 to focus on that skill in one or more of the week's daily paragraphs. To provide additional practice, refer to the Skills Scope & Sequence to find other paragraphs that include the same target skill.

Individual Practice

Once students are familiar with the process for editing the daily paragraphs, they may work on their own or with a partner to make corrections. Be sure students have their Proofreading Marks available to help them mark their corrections. Remind students to refer to the student Language Handbook as needed for guidance in the rules of mechanics and usage. Some students may find it helpful to know at the outset the number and types of errors they are seeking. Provide this information by referring to the Error Summary on the annotated Editing Key pages. You may wish to use a transparency on the overhead to check work with the group. Occasionally, you may wish to assess students' acquisition of skills by collecting and reviewing their work before they check it.

Customizing Instruction

Some of the skills covered in *Daily Paragraph Editing* may not be part of the grade-level expectancies in the language program you use. Some skills may even be taught differently in your program from the way they are modeled in *Daily Paragraph Editing*. In such cases, follow the approach used in your program. Simply revise the paragraph text as needed by covering it with correction fluid or by writing in changes before you reproduce copies for students.

Comma usage is an area where discrepancies are most likely to arise. *Daily Paragraph Editing* uses the "closed" style, where commas are included after short introductory phrases. Except for commas used in salutations, closings, dates, and between city and state in letters, journals, or news articles, all commas that appear in the daily paragraphs have been correctly placed according to the closed style. All other skills related to the use of commas are practiced by requiring students to insert missing commas, rather than moving or deleting extraneous commas.

Occasionally, you or your students may make a correction that differs from that shown in the Editing Key. The decision to use an exclamation mark instead of a period, or a period instead of a semicolon, is often a subjective decision made by individual writers. When discrepancies of this sort arise, capitalize on the "teachable moment" to let students know that there are gray areas in English usage and mechanics, and discuss how each of the possible correct choices can affect the meaning or tone of the writing.

You may wish to have your students mark corrections on the daily paragraphs in a manner that differs from the common proofreading marks on page 10. If so, model the marking style you wish students to follow as you conduct group lessons on an overhead, and point out any differences between the standard proofing marks and those to be used by your students.

Using the Writing Prompts

Have students keep their daily paragraphs in a folder so they can review the week's four corrected paragraphs on Friday. Identify the type of writing modeled in the four-paragraph composition and any of its special features (e.g., dialog in a fictional narrative; salutation, closing, and paragraph style in a letter; opinion statements and supporting arguments in an editorial; etc.).

Present the Friday writing prompt on an overhead transparency, write it on the board, or distribute individual copies to students. Take a few minutes to brainstorm ideas with the group and to focus on language skills that students will need to address in their writing.

After students complete their writing, encourage them to use the Editing Checklist (see page 11) to review or revise their work. You may also wish to have partners review each other's writing. To conduct a more formal assessment of students' writing, use the Assessment Rubric on page 9.

If you assign paragraph writing for homework, be sure students have the week's four corrected paragraphs available as a reference. You may wish to set aside some time for volunteers to read their completed writing to the class, or display compositions on a weekly writing bulletin board for students to enjoy.

Skills Scope and Sequence

Capitalization

Skill / Week No.	1	2	3	4	5	6	7	8	9	10	11	12	13	14	15	16	17	18	19	20	21	22	23	24	25	26	27	28	29	30	31	32	33	34	35	36
Beginning of Sentences, Quotations, Salutations/Closings	•	•	•	•	•	•	•	•	•	•	•	•	•	•	•	•	•	•	•	•	•	•	•	•	•	•	•	•	•	•	•	•	•	•	•	
Days, Months, Holidays		•		•		•										•	•															•	•			
Incorrect Use of Capitals				•		•								•				•																		•
Names & Titles of People, incl. Languages, Nationalities	•		•			•	•		•	•	•				•		•						•			•			•	•		•	•	•		
Names of Places, Historic Events, Organizations	•	•	•			•		•	•	•	•			•	•		•		•		•	•	•				•		•	•			•	•		
Abbreviations of Titles, Organizations													•					•		•	•					•								•		
Nouns Used as Names (Aunt, Grandpa, etc.)											•																	•								•
Titles of Books, Magazines, Poems, Stories													•													•										•

Language Usage

Skill / Week No.	1	2	3	4	5	6	7	8	9	10	11	12	13	14	15	16	17	18	19	20	21	22	23	24	25	26	27	28	29	30	31	32	33	34	35	36
Correct Use of Singular & Plural Forms	•	•	•	•	•	•	•	•	•	•	•	•	•	•	•	•	•	•	•	•	•	•	•	•	•	•	•	•	•	•	•	•	•	•	•	•
Correct Use of Verb Tenses	•		•	•	•	•	•	•	•	•	•	•	•	•	•		•		•	•		•			•	•	•			•		•	•	•	•	
Identify Double Negatives															•									•												•
Use of Correct Adjective & Adverbial Forms						•				•																	•									
Use of Correct Pronouns																•			•																	•

Punctuation: Apostrophes

Skill / Week No.	1	2	3	4	5	6	7	8	9	10	11	12	13	14	15	16	17	18	19	20	21	22	23	24	25	26	27	28	29	30	31	32	33	34	35	36
In Contractions				•	•	•	•	•	•		•	•	•	•	•			•	•	•		•	•		•	•			•	•	•	•	•	•		•
In Possessives	•	•						•	•													•	•					•	•	•			•	•	•	
Improperly Placed														•														•						•	•	•

Punctuation: Commas

Skill / Week No.	1	2	3	4	5	6	7	8	9	10	11	12	13	14	15	16	17	18	19	20	21	22	23	24	25	26	27	28	29	30	31	32	33	34	35	36
After Introductory Dependent Phrase or Clause	•	•	•	•	•	•	•	•	•	•	•	•	•	•	•	•	•	•	•	•	•	•	•	•	•	•	•	•	•	•	•	•	•	•	•	•
After Introductory Interjection or Expression																														•	•				•	
After Salutation & Closing in a Letter							•									•								•												
Between City & State & City & Country Names							•					•						•	•															•		
Between Equally Modifying Adjectives						•			•	•									•											•		•		•		•
Between Items in a Series	•		•					•	•			•			•				•		•	•			•					•	•		•			
In a Date				•	•			•	•	•	•	•	•	•		•																				
To Separate Parts of Compound Sentences	•	•	•	•										•							•				•			•	•	•			•	•	•	•
To Set Off Appositives	•	•												•							•		•									•	•			
To Set Off Interruptions	•			•	•	•		•	•	•					•							•								•	•				•	•
To Set Off Quotations																											•	•								•
With Name Used in Direct Address														•																						•

Skills Scope and Sequence (continued)

8

Week No.

Punctuation: Periods

Skill	1	2	3	4	5	6	7	8	9	10	11	12	13	14	15	16	17	18	19	20	21	22	23	24	25	26	27	28	29	30	31	32	33	34	35	36
After Initials																	•																			
At End of Sentence		•	•	•	•			•	•	•	•	•	•	•	•	•		•	•	•	•	•	•	•	•	•	•	•	•	•	•	•	•	•	•	
In Address Abbreviations																																				
In Time & Measurement Abbreviations									•													•	•	•												
In Title Abbreviations				•				•			•						•			•									•							
To Correct Run-on & Rambling Sentences; Fragments				•								•																								

Punctuation: Quotation Marks

Skill	1	2	3	4	5	6	7	8	9	10	11	12	13	14	15	16	17	18	19	20	21	22	23	24	25	26	27	28	29	30	31	32	33	34	35	36
In Speech												•		•									•				•								•	
To Set Apart Special Words			•	•							•						•			•	•										•			•		•
With Titles of Works of Art, Articles, Poems, Chapters, Short Stories, Songs, Newspaper Articles													•																							

Punctuation: Other

Skill	1	2	3	4	5	6	7	8	9	10	11	12	13	14	15	16	17	18	19	20	21	22	23	24	25	26	27	28	29	30	31	32	33	34	35	36
Exclamation Point		•					•														•													•		
Hyphen in Fractions																				•							•									
Hyphen to Form Adjectives									•			•			•	•		•											•							
Periods & Commas Inside Quotation Marks			•										•				•	•		•											•					•
Question Mark			•	•								•										•							•							
Semicolon to Join Two Independent Clauses														•																						•
Underline Names of Aircraft & Ships								•																								•	•			
Underline Titles of Books, Magazines, Movies, Newspapers, TV Shows										•																		•		•						

Spelling

Skill	1	2	3	4	5	6	7	8	9	10	11	12	13	14	15	16	17	18	19	20	21	22	23	24	25	26	27	28	29	30	31	32	33	34	35	36
Identify Errors in Grade-Level Words	•	•	•	•	•	•	•	•	•	•	•	•	•	•	•	•	•	•	•	•	•	•	•	•	•	•	•	•	•	•	•	•	•	•	•	•

Assessment Rubric for Evaluating Friday Paragraph Writing

The Friday writing prompts give students the opportunity to use the capitalization, punctuation, and other usage and mechanics skills that have been practiced during the week's editing tasks. They also require students to write in a variety of different forms and genres.

In evaluating students' Friday paragraphs, you may wish to focus exclusively on their mastery of the aspects of mechanics and usage targeted that week. However, if you wish to conduct a more global assessment of student writing, the following rubric offers broad guidelines for evaluating the composition as a whole.

Characteristics of Student Writing

	EXCELLENT	GOOD	FAIR	WEAK
Clarity and Focus	Writing is exceptionally clear, focused, and interesting.	Writing is generally clear, focused, and interesting.	Writing is loosely focused on the topic.	Writing is unclear and unfocused.
Development of Main Ideas	Main ideas are clear, specific, and well-developed.	Main ideas are identifiable, but may be somewhat general.	Main ideas are overly broad or simplistic.	Main ideas are unclear or not expressed.
Organization	Organization is clear (beginning, middle, and end) and fits the topic and writing form.	Organization is clear, but may be predictable or formulaic.	Organization is attempted, but is often unclear.	Organization is not coherent.
Use of Details	Details are relevant, specific, and well-placed.	Details are relevant, but may be overly general.	Details may be off-topic, predictable, or not specific enough.	Details are absent or insufficient to support main ideas.
Vocabulary	Vocabulary is exceptionally rich, varied, and well-chosen.	Vocabulary is colorful and generally avoids clichés.	Vocabulary is ordinary and may rely on clichés.	Vocabulary is limited, general, or vague.
Mechanics and Usage	Demonstrates exceptionally strong command of conventions of punctuation, capitalization, spelling, and usage.	Demonstrates control of conventions of punctuation, capitalization, spelling, and usage.	Errors in use of conventions of mechanics and usage distract, but do not impede, the reader.	Limited ability to control conventions of mechanics and usage impairs readability of the composition.

Proofreading Marks

Use these marks to show corrections.

Mark	Meaning	Example
⁹	Take this out (delete).	I love t̶o̶ to read.
⊙	Add a period.	It was late⊙
☰	Make this a capital letter.	First prize went to m̲a̲ria.
/	Make this a lowercase letter.	We saw a B̸lack C̸at.
——	Fix the spelling.	This is our ~~hause~~. (house)
⌄	Add a comma.	Goodnight˄Mom.
⌄	Add an apostrophe.	It˅s mine.
⌄ ⌄	Add quotation marks.	˅Come in, ˅ he said.
! ? ˄ ˄	Add an exclamation point or a question mark.	Help˄! Can you help me˄?
¯˄	Add a hyphen.	Let's go in˄line skating after school.
⌒	Close the space.	Foot‿ball is fun.
˄	Add a word.	The˄pen is mine. (red)
——	Underline the words.	We read <u>Old Yeller</u>.
⌃⌄ ⌃⌄	Add a semicolon or a colon.	Alex arrived at 400 Debbie came later. ˄ ˄

EMC 2728 • Daily Paragraph Editing • ©2004 by Evan-Moor Corp.

Editing Checklist

Use this checklist to review and revise your writing:

◯ Does each sentence begin with a capital letter?

◯ Do names of people and places begin with a capital letter?

◯ Does each sentence end with a period, a question mark, or an exclamation point?

◯ Did I use apostrophes to show possession (*Ana's desk*) and in contractions (*isn't*)?

◯ Did I choose the correct word (*to, too, two*)?

◯ Did I check for spelling errors?

◯ Did I place commas where they are needed?

◯ Are my sentences clear and complete?

Editing Checklist

Use this checklist to review and revise your writing:

◯ Does each sentence begin with a capital letter?

◯ Do names of people and places begin with a capital letter?

◯ Does each sentence end with a period, a question mark, or an exclamation point?

◯ Did I use apostrophes to show possession (*Ana's desk*) and in contractions (*isn't*)?

◯ Did I choose the correct word (*to, too, two*)?

◯ Did I check for spelling errors?

◯ Did I place commas where they are needed?

◯ Are my sentences clear and complete?

Preview the 4 daily lessons to ensure you review or introduce skills that may be unfamiliar to students.

John Muir's Early Life

John muir was born in scotland in 1838. He lived with his family in a small coastal town and ~~begin~~ began his education in the local school. When John was eleven, he moved with his family to the united states. They settled on a farm in wisconsin, and john soon began to help out with the farm ~~choars~~ chores. When he had free time, he loved to wander with his younger brother through the nearby woods, a deep love of nature had begun to awaken in him.

Error Summary	
Capitalization	7
Language Usage	1
Punctuation:	
Comma	3
Period	1
Spelling	1

MONDAY   **WEEK 1**

---

muir was a good student and a creative thinker. by the time he was in his early 20s, he had ~~win~~ won prizes at the state fair for some of his inventions. One of his more unusual creations, for example, was a device that would tip him out of bed each day. Before he ~~finish~~ finished college, muir had the urge to travel. He left school to wander through the northern united states and canada, and he made money along the way by working at ~~od~~ odd jobs.

Error Summary	
Capitalization	6
Language Usage	2
Punctuation:	
Comma	5
Period	2
Spelling	1

TUESDAY   **WEEK 1**

Name _____

John Muir's Early Life

John muir was born in scotland in 1838. He lived with his family in a small coastal town and begin his education in the local school. When John was eleven he moved with his family to the united states. They settled on a farm in wisconsin and john soon began to help out with the farm choars. When he had free time he loved to wander with his younger brother through the nearby woods a deep love of nature had begun to awaken in him.

- commas
- names of places

MONDAY   **WEEK 1**

---

muir was a good student and a creative thinker. by the time he was in his early 20s he had win prizes at the state fair for some of his inventions. One of his more unusual creations for example was a device that would tip him out of bed each day? Before he finish college muir had the urge to travel. He left school to wander through the northern united states and canada and he made money along the way by working at od jobs

- commas

TUESDAY   **WEEK 1**

By the time he was 29 Muir was working at a carriage parts shop in indiana. An ~~axident~~ accident at the shop caused Muir to lose his eyesight. Although his vision returned after a month Muir's short blindness changed his life. He decided to spend more time doing the things that mattered most to him and what he loved most of all ~~were~~ was nature. He began therefore the first of many walking trips, covering 1,000 miles from indiana to the gulf of mexico.

Error Summary

Capitalization	4
Language Usage	1
Punctuation:	
Apostrophe	1
Comma	5
Spelling	1

WEDNESDAY　　　　　　　　　　**WEEK 1**

From the gulf of Mexico Muir continued his journey by ship. He sailed to cuba then on to Panama and finally to california, which became his home. It was not long after his arrival that Muir first hiked in Californias sierra nevada Mountains. He fell in love with their striking beauty and would go on to devote the rest of his life to enjoying, praising and protecting this land. The Sierra club, founded by Muir and others, continues that work today.

Error Summary

Capitalization	6
Punctuation:	
Apostrophe	1
Comma	4
Period	1

THURSDAY　　　　　　　　　　**WEEK 1**

EMC 2728 • *Daily Paragraph Editing, Grade 5* • ©2004 by Evan-Moor Corp.

Name _____

By the time he was 29 Muir was working at a carriage parts shop in indiana. An axident at the shop caused Muir to lose his eyesight. Although his vision returned after a month Muirs short blindness changed his life. He decided to spend more time doing the things that mattered most to him and what he loved most of all were nature. He began therefore the first of many walking trips, covering 1,000 miles from indiana to the gulf of mexico.

• commas

WEDNESDAY   **WEEK 1**

From the gulf of Mexico Muir continued his journey by ship. He sailed to cuba then on to Panama and finally to california, which became his home. It was not long after his arrival that Muir first hiked in Californias sierra nevada Mountains. He fell in love with their striking beauty and would go on to devote the rest of his life to enjoying, praising and protecting this land. The Sierra club, founded by Muir and others, continues that work today

• commas
• names of places

THURSDAY   **WEEK 1**

Preview the 4 daily lessons to ensure you review or introduce skills that may be unfamiliar to students.

My Sister, Dolley Madison

the war that began with great britain two years ago has now reached our doorstep at the beginning of the summer, british troops began to advance on our nations capital. As we now approach the end of august 1814 british soldiers have taken over washington. The White House, home to my sister dolley and president james Madison, her husband has been set afire. with her determined spirit Dolley has been a true heroine?

Error Summary

Capitalization	12
Punctuation:	
Apostrophe	1
Comma	3
Period	2

MONDAY   **WEEK 2**

On august 22, president madison my brother-in-law left the capital to review our troops. The british moved swiftly to take Washington during his absence. on the 23rd, dolley packed important documents into trunks that were carted out of the city. Next, she sent the White house silver to the Bank of maryland for safekeeping. when dolley herself finally escaped she carried little more than the portrait of president Washington

Error Summary

Capitalization	11
Punctuation:	
Comma	3
Period	1

TUESDAY   **WEEK 2**

My Sister, Dolley Madison

the war that began with great britain two years ago has now reached our doorstep at the beginning of the summer, british troops began to advance on our nations capital. As we now approach the end of august 1814 british soldiers have taken over washington. The White House, home to my sister dolley and president james Madison, her husband has been set afire. with her determined spirit Dolley has been a true heroine?

MONDAY   **WEEK 2**

On august 22, president madison my brother-in-law left the capital to review our troops. The british moved swiftly to take Washington during his absence. on the 23rd, dolley packed important documents into trunks that were carted out of the city. Next, she sent the White house silver to the Bank of maryland for safekeeping. when dolley herself finally escaped she carried little more than the portrait of president Washington

TUESDAY   **WEEK 2**

dolley has been an inspiring example of bravery and patriotism for our nation. More than ever before, I find myself bursting with pride at her accomplishments. dolley was already known for her gift of bringing together politicians and diplomats from opposing sides at her popular, festive gatherings. how wonderful it would be if only our conflict with great britain could be resolved at one of dolleys famous social evenings?!

Error Summary	
Capitalization	6
Punctuation:	
Apostrophe	1
Comma	1
Other	1

WEDNESDAY   **WEEK 2**

When will this war be over? it seems there is no end in sight, yet we must find a way to reach an agreement with great britain. After their dreadful looting and burning of our beloved capital city, it is hard to imagine making peace with the british. If ever there has been a leader prepared to meet the difficult demands of wartime negotiation, it is President Madison. with dolleys loyal support, I am confident that he shall lead our nation to peace.

Error Summary	
Capitalization	6
Punctuation:	
Apostrophe	1
Comma	4
Period	2
Other	1
Spelling	2

THURSDAY   **WEEK 2**

Name _____

dolley has been an inspiring example of bravery and patriotism for our nation. More than ever before I find myself bursting with pride at her accomplishments. dolley was already known for her gift of bringing together politicians and diplomats from opposing sides at her popular, festive gatherings. how wonderful it would be if only our conflict with great britain could be resolved at one of dolleys famous social evenings?

• exclamation points

WEDNESDAY　　　　　　　　　　**WEEK 2**

When will this war be over. it seems there is no end in sight yet we must find a way to reach an agreement with great britain. After there dreadful looting and burning of our beloved capital city it is hard to imagine making piece with the british. If ever there has been a leader prepared to meet the difficult demands of wartime negotiation it is President Madison with dolleys loyal support I am confident that he shall lead our nation to peace

• commas

THURSDAY　　　　　　　　　　**WEEK 2**

Preview the 4 daily lessons to ensure you review or introduce skills that may be unfamiliar to students.

Summer Solstice

all around the world the seasons change and the weather changes, too. snow rain and lower temperatures in many places indicate the arrival of Old Man Winter." Summer, on the other hand is a season with warm temperatures sunny days and night skies that is (are) reluctant to grow dark. why does the sun stay up longer and the moon come out later during the summer? Learning about the summer solstice may help you to understand

Error Summary	
Capitalization	3
Language Usage	1
Punctuation:	
Comma	7
Period	1
Quotation Mark	1
Other	1

MONDAY   **WEEK 3**

there is one day each year when the sun stays up longer than any other day this day is known as summer solstice It is the longest day of the year and it marks the begining (beginning) of summer in the Northern Hemisphere Summer solstice occurs around June 21st when the position of the sun is as far north as it ever gets during the year Because the sun is above the horizon longer than it is during winter it provides daylight for a longer amount of time

Error Summary	
Capitalization	2
Punctuation:	
Comma	2
Period	5
Spelling	1

TUESDAY   **WEEK 3**

Summer Solstice

all around the world the seasons change and the weather changes, too. snow rain and lower temperatures in many places indicate the arrival of Old Man Winter." Summer, on the other hand is a season with warm temperatures sunny days and night skies that is reluctant to grow dark. why does the sun stay up longer and the moon come out later during the summer Learning about the summer solstice may help you to understand

MONDAY	WEEK 3

there is one day each year when the sun stays up longer than any other day this day is known as summer solstice It is the longest day of the year and it marks the begining of summer in the Northern Hemisphere Summer solstice occurs around June 21st when the position of the sun is as far north as it ever gets during the year Because the sun is above the horizon longer than it is during winter it provides daylight for a longer amount of time

TUESDAY	WEEK 3

once summer begins the sun starts to rise a little farther south each day for the next six months in the northern hemisphere this marks the seasons of summer and fall By late fall the hours of sunlight have ~~begin~~ begun to dwindle as the shortest day of the year, known as winter solstice, approaches That day which is usually December 21ˢᵗ marks the beginning of summer solstice in the southern hemisphere.

WEDNESDAY   **WEEK 3**

So what does the word "solstice" mean? it is a latin word that means "the sun stood still During the summer and winter solstices the sun appears to rise and set at almost exactly the same places that it has in previous years. this makes it easy to predict when the seasons will change and what kind of ~~whether~~ weather to expect many people spend the summer solstice the longest day of the year enjoying the warm sunshine with a day on the beach and a bonfire.

THURSDAY   **WEEK 3**

Name _____

once summer begins the sun starts to rise a little farther south each day for the next six months in the northern hemisphere this marks the seasons of summer and fall By late fall the hours of sunlight have begin to dwindle as the shortest day of the year, known as winter solstice, approaches That day which is usually December 21st marks the beginning of summer solstice in the southern hemisphere.

• commas

WEDNESDAY   **WEEK 3**

So what does the word "solstice" mean it is a latin word that means "the sun stood still During the summer and winter solstices the sun appears to rise and set at almost exactly the same places that it has in previous years. this makes it easy to predict when the seasons will change and what kind of whether to expect many people spend the summer solstice the longest day of the year enjoying the warm sunshine with a day on the beach and a bonfire.

• commas

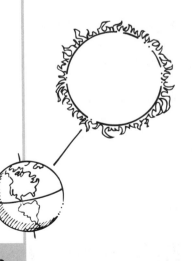

THURSDAY   **WEEK 3**

Preview the 4 daily lessons to ensure you review or introduce skills that may be unfamiliar to students.

Bring Back "Pizza Thursdays"

Did you notice all the complaining grumbling and discontent in the cafeteria last thursday? As one class after another arrived to eat lunch students expresses ~~expressed~~ disappointment that there would be no "Pizza thursday." although it may not have been obvious before it should be clear to everybody now that the students at lark creek elementary school have gotten very ~~attatched~~ *attached* to the idea of eating pizza for lunch on thursdays

MONDAY   **WEEK 4**

Error Summary

Capitalization	8
Language Usage	1
Punctuation:	
Comma	4
Period	1
Other	1
Spelling	1

Mrs lee the cafeteria manager pointed out that pizza will now be served every other thursday. she said this change was made in order to keep the pizza lunches a special occasion for students mrs lee said "it seemed to us that serving the same food each week would get ~~boaring~~ *boring*. We really thought this change would help Make the pizza lunches more special. The ~~knew~~ *new* schedule went into effect this week

TUESDAY   **WEEK 4**

Error Summary

Capitalization	7
Punctuation:	
Comma	3
Period	5
Quotation Mark	1
Spelling	2

EMC 2728 • Daily Paragraph Editing, Grade 5 • ©2004 by Evan-Moor Corp.

Name _____

Bring Back "Pizza Thursdays"

- commas
- names of places

Did you notice all the complaining grumbling and discontent in the cafeteria last thursday. As one class after another arrived to eat lunch students expresses disappointment that there would be no "Pizza thursday." although it may not have been obvious before it should be clear to everybody now that the students at lark creek elementary school have gotten very attatched to the idea of eating pizza for lunch on thursdays

MONDAY	**WEEK 4**

Mrs lee the cafeteria manager pointed out that pizza will now be served every other thursday. she said this change was made in order to keep the pizza lunches a special occasion for students mrs lee said "it seemed to us that serving the same food each week would get boaring. We really thought this change would help. Make the pizza lunches more special. The knew schedule went into effect this week

- quotes
- abbreviations

TUESDAY	**WEEK 4**

　　　Reporters for the school paper the <u>Lark creek</u>
<u>Chronicle</u>, talked to ~~kid~~ (kids) in every grade about the
new schedule. When asked, "Is it more special to
have pizza every thursday, or every other thursday?"
the students surveyed said they prefer weekly pizza
menus. Some offered suggestions, such as, "To keep
the pizza menu interesting, vary the toppings. We
could have cheese one week pepperoni the next and
then mushroom."

Error Summary

Capitalization	3
Language Usage	1
Punctuation:	
Comma	3
Period	1
Quotation Mark	1
Other	2

WEDNESDAY　　　　　　　　**WEEK 4**

　　　It's great that the cafeteria staff wants
to keep the lunch menu varied interesting and
kid-friendly. If you really want to please the lark
creek students please listen to our opinions. We
prefer "Pizza thursdays" every week pizza is a healthy
food. It is a food that can be easily varied. From
one week to another. Come on Lark creek cafeteria!
Let's make this a win-win situation Restore our ~~weakly~~ (weekly)
"pizza thursdays"!

Error Summary

Capitalization	8
Punctuation:	
Apostrophe	2
Comma	4
Period	3
Quotation Mark	2
Spelling	1

THURSDAY　　　　　　　　**WEEK 4**

Name _____

Reporters for the school paper the Lark creek Chronicle, talked to kid in every grade about the new schedule. When asked, Is it more special to have pizza every thursday, or every other thursday" the students surveyed said they prefer weekly pizza menus. Some offered suggestions, such as, "To keep the pizza menu interesting, vary the toppings. We could have cheese one week pepperoni the next and then mushroom"

WATCH FOR
- quotes
- commas

WEDNESDAY	**WEEK 4**

Its great that the cafeteria staff wants to keep the lunch menu varied interesting and kid-friendly. If you really want to please the lark creek students please listen to our opinions. We prefer Pizza thursdays every week pizza is a healthy food. It is a food that can be easily varied. From one week to another. Come on Lark creek cafeteria! Lets make this a win-win situation Restore our weakly "pizza thursdays"!

WATCH FOR
- apostrophes
- commas

THURSDAY	**WEEK 4**

Preview the 4 daily lessons to ensure you review or introduce skills that may be unfamiliar to students.

The Business of Farming

In many parts of the world farming is a very big bisness. these days, farmers needs to know more [business] [need] than just how to plant a seed? They need to know how to plan ahead how machines work what soil conditions make plants grow well, and how to keep track of money. in order to plan their year farmers must know what crops people will buy. they must study government reports and other materials to help them make decisions about what to groe [grow]

Error Summary	
Capitalization	3
Language Usage	1
Punctuation:	
Comma	4
Period	2
Spelling	2

MONDAY   **WEEK 5**

some crops require specific kinds of machines to plant cultivate, or harvest farmers must decide which machines to buy or rent. each year, farmers use money earned from the previous years crops to buy or rent any special machinery that is needed. In addition to special machinery, many crops require speicial soil conditions? fertilizer chemicals, or other [special] soil additives must sometimes be buyed to improve [bought] the soil

Error Summary	
Capitalization	4
Language Usage	1
Punctuation:	
Apostrophe	1
Comma	4
Period	3
Spelling	1

TUESDAY   **WEEK 5**

EMC 2728 • Daily Paragraph Editing, Grade 5 • ©2004 by Evan-Moor Corp.

Name _____

The Business of Farming

In many parts of the world farming is a very big bisness. these days, farmers needs to know more than just how to plant a seed? They need to know how to plan ahead how machines work what soil conditions make plants grow well, and how to keep track of money. in order to plan their year farmers must know what crops people will buy. they must study government reports and other materials to help them make decisions about what to groe

MONDAY	**WEEK 5**

some crops require specific kinds of machines to plant cultivate, or harvest farmers must decide which machines to buy or rent. each year, farmers use money earned from the previous years crops to buy or rent any special machinery that is needed. In addition to special machinery many crops require speicial soil conditions? fertilizer chemicals or other soil additives must sometimes be buyed to improve the soil

TUESDAY	**WEEK 5**

Once farmers have ~~chose~~ (chosen) which crops to plant, they must also ~~deside~~ (decide) how to keep them healthy. Bugs and other pests can damage or destroy crops. weeds can deprive crops of nutrients, water, and sunlight. Some farmers solve these problems by using ~~kemicals~~ (chemicals) to kill bugs and weeds. Many of these chemicals can help crops stay healthy, but those that remain active for a long time can build up in the environment. this can pollute water and soil.

Error Summary

Capitalization	2
Language Usage	1
Punctuation:	
Comma	4
Period	2
Spelling	2

WEDNESDAY   **WEEK 5**

Some farmers choose natural solutions for their problems. For example, they plant cover crops. later, the cover crops are tilled into the fields, enriching the soil without using chemicals. helpful insects are ~~bringed~~ (brought) in to eat pests. Weeds are controlled with tractors or hand tools. farmers must decide on the best method and choose to spend their ~~ernings~~ (earnings) on chemicals, machinery, or natural methods. Farmers must know about both business and science.

Error Summary

Capitalization	3
Language Usage	1
Punctuation:	
Comma	2
Period	4
Spelling	1

THURSDAY   **WEEK 5**

Name _____

Once farmers have chose which crops to plant they must also deside how to keep them healthy Bugs and other pests can damage or destroy crops. weeds can deprive crops of nutrients water and sunlight. Some farmers solve these problems by using kemicals to kill bugs and weeds. Many of these chemicals can help crops stay healthy but those that remain active for a long time can build up in the environment. this can pollute water and soil

- commas

WEDNESDAY   **WEEK 5**

Some farmers choose natural solutions for their problems. For example, they plant cover crops later, the cover crops are tilled into the fields, enriching the soil without using chemicals helpful insects are bringed in to eat pests. Weeds are controlled with tractors or hand tools farmers must decide on the best method and choose to spend their ernings on chemicals machinery or natural methods. Farmers must know about both business and science

- run-on sentences

THURSDAY   **WEEK 5**

Preview the 4 daily lessons to ensure you review or introduce skills that may be unfamiliar to students.

"Pap" Singleton: A Man with a Dream

After the Civil War african Americans in the South were freed from slavery but they were still terribly ~~pore~~ poor. One of these former slaves was a man ~~name~~ named Benjamin singleton. He wanted to help himself and he also wanted to help others facing similar challenges Singleton organized a group of black farmers to buy land together in tennessee but white landowners would not sell to them at fair prices. singleton however was not willing to give up

MONDAY   **WEEK 6**

Error Summary

Capitalization	4
Language Usage	1
Punctuation:	
Comma	6
Period	2
Spelling	1

---

singleton heard about new opportunities in kansas There was plenty of land available but not many people to work it. Settlers were encouraged to come help develop this open fertile country. rumors ~~spred~~ spread about free tools seeds and plows for all who would work the land. Singleton knew these were false appealing reports He still believed that former slaves could make promising better lives for themselves if they only had the chance to own land

TUESDAY   **WEEK 6**

Error Summary

Capitalization	3
Punctuation:	
Comma	5
Period	3
Spelling	1

EMC 2728 • Daily Paragraph Editing, Grade 5 • ©2004 by Evan-Moor Corp.

Name _____

"Pap" Singleton: A Man with a Dream

• commas

After the Civil War african Americans in the South were freed from slavery but they were still terribly pore. One of these former slaves was a man name Benjamin singleton. He wanted to help himself and he also wanted to help others facing similar challenges Singleton organized a group of black farmers to buy land together in tennessee but white landowners would not sell to them at fair prices. singleton however was not willing to give up

MONDAY   **WEEK 6**

• commas

singleton heard about new opportunities in kansas There was plenty of land available but not many people to work it. Settlers were encouraged to come help develop this open fertile country. rumors spred about free tools seeds and plows for all who would work the land. Singleton knew these were false appealing reports He still believed that former slaves could make promising better lives for themselves if they only had the chance to own land

TUESDAY   **WEEK 6**

It was not hard for singleton to persuade people from the south to follow him to kansas. Although black people in the South were free, they still were not treated well. they were forced to live as second-class citizens. groups like the Ku Klux Klan formed at this time. they used violence, threats, and fear to keep black people from moving into new roles in society. Its no surprise that more than 50,000 african americans left the south in the late 1870s

Error Summary	
Capitalization	9
Punctuation:	
Apostrophe	1
Comma	3
Period	2

WEDNESDAY   **WEEK 6**

"Pap" singleton, as he was known, founded ~~to~~ two different settlements in kansas. Many who followed him to kansas became established, successful farmers. their dreams came true. singleton, however, had other dreams to pursue. He started a political party that worked to help the black community set up businesses, factories ~~factorys~~ and other industries. singleton did not live to see this dream come true, but others helped keep ~~kept~~ his dream alive

Error Summary	
Capitalization	6
Language Usage	1
Punctuation:	
Comma	6
Period	1
Spelling	2

THURSDAY   **WEEK 6**

Name _____

It was not hard for singleton to persuade people from the south to follow him to kansas. Although black people in the South were free they still were not treated well they were forced to live as second-class citizens. groups like the Ku Klux Klan formed at this time. they used violence threats and fear to keep black people from moving into new roles in society. Its no surprise that more than 50,000 african americans left the south in the late 1870s

• names of people
• names of places

WEDNESDAY   **WEEK 6**

"Pap" singleton, as he was known, founded to different settlements in kansas. Many who followed him to kansas became established successful farmers. their dreams came true. singleton however had other dreams to pursue. He started a political party that worked to help the black community set up businesses factorys and other industries. singleton did not live to see this dream come true but others helped kept his dream alive

• commas

THURSDAY   **WEEK 6**

Preview the 4 daily lessons to ensure you review or introduce skills that may be unfamiliar to students.

Foreign Exchange

Chicago, illinois
june 12, 2004

dear kyoko,

    I just learned that you will be ~~come~~ *coming* to live with my family this summer. I ~~is~~ *am* so excited! The people at the Student exchange Office ~~says~~ *say* that you will be here in two ~~weaks~~ *weeks* I hope this letter reaches you before you leave your home in japan.

Error Summary	
Capitalization	6
Language Usage	3
Punctuation:	
Comma	3
Period	2
Spelling	1

MONDAY   **WEEK 7**

    Let me tell you a little bit about our home. my mother ~~work~~ *works* in a school office, so she is on vacation this summer. my dad paints houses, so summer is a busy time for him. my older sister has left home to go to college, so you and I will be the only "children" in the family I ~~looked~~ *look* forward to meeting you. best wishes to you.

    your american "sister"
    Anicka

Error Summary	
Capitalization	6
Language Usage	2
Punctuation:	
Comma	4
Period	3

TUESDAY   **WEEK 7**

          EMC 2728 • Daily Paragraph Editing, Grade 5 • ©2004 by Evan-Moor Corp.

Foreign Exchange

Chicago illinois

june 12 2004

dear kyoko

    I just learned that you will be come to live with my family this summer. I is so excited! The people at the Student exchange Office says that you will be here in two weaks I hope this letter reaches you before you leave your home in japan

MONDAY   **WEEK 7**

    Let me tell you a little bit about our home. my mother work in a school office so she is on vacation this summer. my dad paints houses so summer is a busy time for him. my older sister has left home to go to college so you and I will be the only "children" in the family I looked forward to meeting you best wishes to you

    your american "sister"

    Anicka

TUESDAY   **WEEK 7**

Kamakura, japan

june 18, 2004

Dear anicka,

    How ~~exiting~~ (exciting) to get a letter from my american

sister?! It is even more exciting to think that in a

week I will be meeting you and staying at your house!

Thank you for welcoming me. This will be the first

time that I ~~am~~ (will be) away from home for so long.

Error Summary

Capitalization	4
Language Usage	2
Punctuation:	
Comma	2
Period	1
Other	1
Spelling	1

    during the summer I usually ~~spending~~ (spend) many hours

on the beaches of kamakura I will no doubt, spend

many hours this summer studying english and doing

schoolwork, but it will be fun to do it in chicago.

It will also be very nice for me to have a sister

In my family, I am the only daughter.

    we will speak in person soon Until then,

best wishes.

    your japanese sister,

Kyoko

Error Summary

Capitalization	7
Language Usage	1
Punctuation:	
Comma	5
Period	4

Kamakura japan

june 18, 2004

- letter (greeting)
- verb tenses

Dear anicka

How exiting to get a letter from my american sister? It is even more exciting to think that in a week I will meeting you and staying at your house! Thank you for welcoming me. This will be the first time that I am away from home for so long

WEDNESDAY   **WEEK 7**

during the summer I usually spending many hours on the beaches of kamakura I will no doubt spend many hours this summer studying english and doing schoolwork but it will be fun to do it in chicago. It will also be very nice for me to have a sister In my family, I am the only daughter.

we will speak in person soon Until then, best wishes

your japanese sister

Kyoko

- letter (closing)
- commas

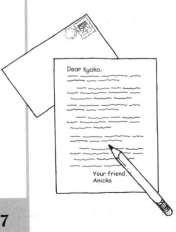

Dear Kyoko,

Your friend,
Anicka

THURSDAY   **WEEK 7**

Preview the 4 daily lessons to ensure you review or introduce skills that may be unfamiliar to students.

Trade Route to India

July 8, 1497

The ruler of portugal, King manuel I vested Vasco da Gama, our captain-major with a fleet of four vessels. I am aboard the Berrio the third vessel in Capt. da Gamas fleet. the largest vessel the São Gabriel is the lead ship. the São Raphael follows, and we are next. Last is the tiny fourth ship that carries all the food. We are charged with establishing a trade route to india.

Error Summary	
Capitalization	5
Punctuation:	
Apostrophe	1
Comma	7
Period	1
Other	1

MONDAY   **WEEK 8**

November 7, 1497

I have been at sea for many fortnights, and we have not yet reached our destination. presently, we have cast anchor in the Bay of Saint Helena. we will remain here for eight days, but it doesnt seem long enough to finish our work. we must mend the sails, clean out the hold, and take in wood and food. I am part of a crew of thirty sailors. There is enough work, however, for at least fifty men.

Error Summary	
Capitalization	3
Punctuation:	
Apostrophe	1
Comma	6
Period	2

TUESDAY   **WEEK 8**

EMC 2728 • Daily Paragraph Editing, Grade 5 • ©2004 by Evan-Moor Corp.

Trade Route to India

- names of ships
- commas

July 8: 1497

The ruler of portugal King manuel I vested Vasco da Gama, our captain-major with a fleet of four vessels. I am aboard the <u>Berrio</u> the third vessel in Capt. da Gamas fleet. the largest vessel the <u>São Gabriel</u> is the lead ship. the São Raphael follows, and we are next. Last is the tiny fourth ship that carries all the food. We are charged with establishing a trade route to india

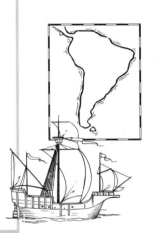

MONDAY   **WEEK 8**

November 7= 1497

- commas

I have been at sea for many fortnights and we have not yet reached our destination. presently, we have cast anchor in the Bay of Saint Helena. we will remain here for eight days but it doesnt seem long enough to finish our work we must mend the sails clean out the hold and take in wood and food. I am part of a crew of thirty sailors. There is enough work, however for at least fifty men

TUESDAY   **WEEK 8**

november 12, 1497

we have been working tirelessly for many days Our duties are difficult but the weather thankfully has been most agreeable Many birds fly overhead and circle our ships looking for food. I have seen cormorants gulls turtle doves crested larks and many others. natives laden with offerings approached our ships. When they were a stones throw away we alerted capt. da gama

Error Summary

Capitalization	5
Punctuation:	
Apostrophe	1
Comma	6
Period	3

WEDNESDAY   **WEEK 8**

november 13, 1497

My closest comrade jorge is posted to Capt da gamas vessel, the <u>São Gabriel</u>. he witnessed capt. da Gamas encounter with the natives they offered the captain cinnamon cloves seed-pearls gold and many other treasures As we travel farther up the african coast will ~~citys~~ cities such as Mozambique mombasa and malindi offer such riches?

Error Summary

Capitalization	9
Punctuation:	
Apostrophe	2
Comma	10
Period	3
Other	2
Spelling	1

THURSDAY   **WEEK 8**

Name _____

november 12, 1497

we have been working tirelessly for many days Our duties are difficult but the weather thankfully has been most agreeable Many birds fly overhead and circle our ships looking for food. I have seen cormorants gulls turtle doves crested larks and many others. natives laden with offerings approached our ships. When they were a stones throw away we alerted capt. da gama

• commas

WEDNESDAY   **WEEK 8**

november 13: 1497

My closest comrade jorge is posted to Capt da gamas vessel, the São Gabriel. he witnessed capt. da Gamas encounter with the natives they offered the captain cinnamon cloves seed-pearls gold and many other treasures As we travel farther up the african coast will citys such as Mozambique mombasa and malindi offer such riches

• names of ships
• commas

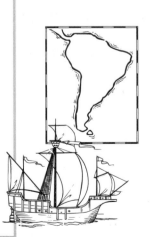

THURSDAY   **WEEK 8**

Preview the 4 daily lessons to ensure you review or introduce skills that may be unfamiliar to students.

Busy as a Beaver

have you ever wondered where the expression "busy as a beaver" comes from? people use this saying because beavers ~~is~~ (are) always working beavers, in fact are one of the few animals that change the natural environment to better suit their needs. a beaver ~~familee~~ (family) works together to build a dam that changes the course of a stream the dam also creates a pond Next, they build their underwater home, called a lodge or a den

Error Summary	
Capitalization	5
Language Usage	1
Punctuation:	
Comma	1
Period	4
Other	1
Spelling	1

MONDAY   **WEEK 9**

~~Bilding~~ (Building) a beaver lodge is hard work. North Americas largest rodent however has a body well suited for underwater activity. beavers have transparent eyelids that act as goggles to protect their eyes underwater They can close off their nose ears and throat to keep the water out. Their powerful webbed back feet make them excellent swimmers their coarse heavy fur ~~are~~ (is) waterproof. Their broad sharp front teeth can cut and carry wood

Error Summary	
Capitalization	2
Language Usage	1
Punctuation:	
Apostrophe	1
Comma	7
Period	3
Other	1
Spelling	1

TUESDAY   **WEEK 9**

EMC 2728 • Daily Paragraph Editing, Grade 5 • ©2004 by Evan-Moor Corp.

Busy as a Beaver

have you ever wondered where the expression "busy as a beaver" comes from people use this saying because beavers is always working beavers, in fact are one of the few animals that change the natural environment to better suit their needs. a beaver familee works together to build a dam that changes the course of a stream the dam also creates a pond Next, they build their underwater home, called a lodge or a den

MONDAY	WEEK 9

Bilding a beaver lodge is hard work. North Americas largest rodent however has a body well_suited for underwater activity. beavers have transparent eyelids that act as goggles to protect their eyes underwater They can close off their nose ears and throat to keep the water out. Their powerful webbed back feet make them excellent swimmers their coarse heavy fur are waterproof. Their broad sharp front teeth can cut and carry wood

TUESDAY	WEEK 9

beaver families usually ~~has~~ *have* two adults and two to six young beavers, called kits family members may work together to build the lodge. the ~~families~~ dome-shaped lodge is built partially underwater. It is made of sticks and rocks that are plastered together with mud beavers use their broad powerful teeth to carry sticks their five-fingered clawed paws are used to scoop up mud the top of the completed lodge reaches about 3 ft above water

Error Summary	
Capitalization	6
Language Usage	1
Punctuation:	
Comma	2
Period	6
Other	2
Spelling	1

WEDNESDAY WEEK 9

Doesnt it seem incredible that these rodents can make such an impact on their environment the average beaver after all is only about 3 ft long its flat thick tail is about 1 ft long. These herbivores or plant eaters usually ~~way~~ *weigh* about 44 lbs, but they can reach up to 77 lbs It takes a lot of grass leaves twigs and bark to power up one of natures busiest creatures!

Error Summary	
Capitalization	2
Punctuation:	
Apostrophe	2
Comma	8
Period	5
Other	1
Spelling	1

THURSDAY WEEK 9

EMC 2728 • Daily Paragraph Editing, Grade 5 • ©2004 by Evan-Moor Corp.

beaver families usually has two adults and two to six young beavers, called kits family members may work together to build the lodge. the families dome=shaped lodge is built partially underwater. It is made of sticks and rocks that are plastered together with mud beavers use their broad powerful teeth to carry sticks their five/fingered clawed paws are used to scoop up mud the top of the completed lodge reaches about 3 ft above water

WATCH FOR

- hyphens
- run-on sentences

WEDNESDAY   **WEEK 9**

Doesnt it seem incredible that these rodents can make such an impact on their environment the average beaver after all is only about 3 ft long its flat thick tail is about 1 ft long. These herbivores or plant eaters usually way about 44 lbs, but they can reach up to 77 lbs It takes a lot of grass leaves twigs and bark to power up one of natures busiest creatures!

WATCH FOR

- abbreviations
- commas

THURSDAY   **WEEK 9**

Preview the 4 daily lessons to ensure you review or introduce skills that may be unfamiliar to students.

How to Build a Sand Castle

building a sand castle can be tricky if you dig a hole too close to the shoreline the castle may get washed out by waves If you are ~~two~~ _{too} far from the shore you will have to dig a very deep hole in order to reach wet sand however for ^{an} a~~~~ almost perfect sand ^{castle} ~~castel~~ just follow the guidelines below

Error Summary

Capitalization	3
Language Usage	1
Punctuation:	
Comma	4
Period	4
Spelling	2

MONDAY   **WEEK 10**

---

after choosing a good spot dig a hole and place the scooped-out sand next to it The deeper you dig the more moisture the sand will have. fill a ^{bucket} ~~buket~~ with seawater and keep it next to your hole. you are now ready to start building your sand castle. Remember, building a sand castle requires patience and a steady hand. of course it always helps to have sand with just the right amount of moisture

Error Summary

Capitalization	4
Punctuation:	
Comma	3
Period	2
Spelling	1

TUESDAY   **WEEK 10**

How to Build a Sand Castle

building a sand castle can be tricky if you dig a hole too close to the shoreline the castle may get washed out by waves If you are two far from the shore you will have to dig a very deep hole in order to reach wet sand however for a almost perfect sand castel just follow the guidelines below

- run-on sentences
- commas

MONDAY   **WEEK 10**

---

after choosing a good spot dig a hole and place the scooped-out sand next to it The deeper you dig the more moisture the sand will have. fill a buket with seawater and keep it next to your hole. you are now ready to start building your sand castle. Remember, building a sand castle requires patience and a steady hand. of course it always helps to have sand with just the right amount of moisture

- run-on sentences

TUESDAY   **WEEK 10**

start by using moist sand to make a flat, even base for your castle. Next, use more of this sand to build layers think of how a grand, layered wedding cake is stacked with each layer getting smaller as it reaches the top the easiest way to do this is to sprinkle handfuls of sand onto the base, and then gently flatten them and mold them into a circular shape each layer should have a smaller circumference than the previous one

Error Summary

Capitalization	4
Punctuation:	
Comma	3
Period	4
Spelling	1

WEDNESDAY   **WEEK 10**

next, use wet sand to even out and smooth the tower layers Finally, you are ready to build the walls use your bucket of seawater to wet some sand. Be sure not to let the water or wet sand touch the tower first, grab a handful of sand and flatten it between your palms use your hands to shape it into a brick or block Next, place the sand brick about six inches away from the tower make more sand bricks and place them side by side, creating a circle around the tower. now, stand back and admire your sand castle

Error Summary

Capitalization	6
Punctuation:	
Period	7
Spelling	1

THURSDAY   **WEEK 10**

EMC 2728 • Daily Paragraph Editing, Grade 5 • ©2004 by Evan-Moor Corp.

Name _____

start by using moist sand to make a flat even base for your castle. Next, use more of this sand to bild layers think of how a grand layered wedding cake is stacked with each layer getting smaller as it reaches the top the easiest way to do this is to sprinkle handfuls of sand onto the base and then gently flatten them and mold them into a circular shape each layer should have a smaller circumference than the previous one

• run-on sentences

WEDNESDAY   **WEEK 10**

next, use wet sand to even out and smooth the tower layers Finally, you are ready to build the walls use your bucket of seawater to wet some sand. Be sure not to let the watter or wet sand touch the tower first, grab a handful of sand and flatten it between your palms use your hands to shape it into a brick or block Next, place the sand brick about six inches away from the tower make more sand bricks and place them side by side, creating a circle around the tower. now, stand back and admire your sand castle

• run-on sentences

THURSDAY   **WEEK 10**

Preview the 4 daily lessons to ensure you review or introduce skills that may be unfamiliar to students.

A Magical Journey

The Lion, the Witch, and the Wardrobe, written by C.S. Lewis takes readers on a magical journey to the land of Narnia Peter Susan edmond and lucy are visiting Professor kirks country home While exploring the house Lucy the youngest of the four children finds an enormous wardrobe. She discovers that the back of the wardrobe leads her into the strange land of narnia after having tea with a fawn named Tumnus Lucy returns home

MONDAY　　　　　　　　　　**WEEK 11**

Error Summary

Capitalization	5
Punctuation:	
Apostrophe	1
Comma	8
Period	4

when Lucy arrives home she tells peter susan and edmond about her adventure in the wardrobe. No one except professor kirk believes her When edmond decides to explore the back of the wardrobe he also enters the land of narnia. Edmond immediately meets the White Witch, otherwise known as the "Queen of Narnia She entices edmond to try a special sweet called "Turkish Delight, which he then begins to crave.

TUESDAY　　　　　　　　　　**WEEK 11**

Error Summary

Capitalization	8
Punctuation:	
Comma	4
Period	2
Quotation Mark	2

Name _____

A Magical Journey

- commas
- apostrophes

The Lion, the Witch, and the Wardrobe, written by C.S. Lewis takes readers on a magical journey to the land of Narnia Peter Susan edmond and lucy are visiting Professor kirks country home While exploring the house Lucy the youngest of the four children finds an enormous wardrobe. She discovers that the back of the wardrobe leads her into the strange land of narnia after having tea with a fawn named Tumnus Lucy returns home

MONDAY   **WEEK 11**

- names of people
- special words in quotes

when Lucy arrives home she tells peter susan and edmond about her adventure in the wardrobe. No one except professor kirk believes her When edmond decides to explore the back of the wardrobe he also enters the land of narnia. Edmond immediately meets the White Witch, otherwise known as the "Queen of Narnia She entices edmond to try a special sweet called "Turkish Delight, which he then begins to crave.

TUESDAY   **WEEK 11**

eventually, all four children enter the land of narnia during their adventures they meet many interesting characters. some are good and some are evil you will have to read The lion, the Witch and the wardrobe to find out whether Aslan, otherwise known as the "King of Narnia, mr and mrs Beaver Dwarf Maugrin, Father Christmas and Tumnas are good or evil. peter susan edmond and lucy had to find out the hard way

Error Summary

Capitalization	13
Punctuation:	
Comma	7
Period	5
Quotation Mark	1
Other	1

WEDNESDAY   **WEEK 11**

if you enjoy tales of adventure and suspense you will surely want to read the rest of the books about Narnia. The Magicians Nephew is the prequel to The lion, the witch, and the wardrobe, which is followed by The Horse and His Boy. The other four books in this exciting series are Prince Caspian, Voyage of the Dawn Treader, The Silver Chair, and The Last Battle. Step into narnia, readers if you dare!

Error Summary

Capitalization	5
Punctuation:	
Apostrophe	1
Comma	2
Other	7

THURSDAY   **WEEK 11**

EMC 2728 • Daily Paragraph Editing, Grade 5 • ©2004 by Evan-Moor Corp.

eventually, all four children enter the land of narnia during their adventures they meet many interesting characters. some are good and some are evil you will have to read The lion, the Witch and the wardrobe to find out whether Aslan, otherwise known as the "King of Narnia, mr and mrs Beaver Dwarf Maugrin, Father Christmas and Tumnas are good or evil. peter susan edmond and lucy had to find out the hard way

WATCH FOR

- book titles
- run-on sentences

WEDNESDAY   **WEEK 11**

if you enjoy tales of adventure and suspense you will surely want to read the rest of the books about Narnia. The Magicians Nephew is the prequel to The lion, the witch, and the wardrobe, which is followed by The Horse and His Boy. The other four books in this exciting series are Prince Caspian, Voyage of the Dawn Treader, The Silver Chair, and The Last Battle. Step into narnia, readers if you dare!

WATCH FOR

- book titles

The Lion, the Witch, and the Wardrobe

THURSDAY   **WEEK 11**

Preview the 4 daily lessons to ensure you review or introduce skills that may be unfamiliar to students.

New Baseball Record Set

St. louis missouri　　　　　　　september, 29, 1998

last night, a powerful swing from mark McGwire's bat. Sent his 70th home run of the season out of the park, setting a remarkable new baseball record. McGwire had already broke (broken) babe Ruths record of 60 home runs set in 1927 when the "Sultan of swat" played for the new york Yankees. Only roger Maris had exceeded that mark, hitting 61 home runs in 1961

Error Summary

Capitalization	11
Language Usage	1
Punctuation:	
Apostrophe	1
Comma	2
Period	3

MONDAY　　　　　　　　　　　　WEEK 12

At busch Stadium the st. louis cardinals home park, the capacity crowd went wild when mcGwire smashed a powerful soaring drive over the wall. The game was interrupted by a roaring standing ovation as the crowd cheer (cheered) in celebration the scene had been the same on September 8th when Mcgwire broke maris's record of 61 homers. that game was delayed while mcGwire hugged his family and other fans.

Error Summary

Capitalization	10
Language Usage	1
Punctuation:	
Apostrophe	1
Comma	4
Period	1

TUESDAY　　　　　　　　　　　　WEEK 12

EMC 2728 • Daily Paragraph Editing, Grade 5 • ©2004 by Evan-Moor Corp.

Name _____

New Baseball Record Set

St louis missouri   september, 29 1998

    last night, a powerful swing from mark McGwire's bat. Sent his 70th home run of the season out of the park, setting a remarkable new baseball record. McGwire had already broke babe Ruths record of 60 home runs set in 1927 when the "Sultan of swat" played for the new york Yankees. Only roger Maris had exceeded that mark, hitting 61 home runs in 1961

- names of people
- names of places
- names of sports teams

MONDAY   **WEEK 12**

    At busch Stadium the st. louis cardinals home park the capacity crowd went wild when mcGwire smashed a powerful soaring drive over the wall. The game was interrupted by a roaring standing ovation as the crowd cheer in celebration the scene had been the same on September 8th when Mcgwire broke maris's record of 61 homers. that game was delayed while mcGwire hugged his family and other fans.

- names of people
- names of places
- names of sports teams
- commas

TUESDAY   **WEEK 12**

when asked about his reaction to this once-in-a-lifetime historic event, McGwire said "to say the least, Im amazed. I can't believe I did it can you? It blows me away!

McGwire is not the only one ~~whose~~ who's amazed. fans have been flocking to the ballpark in record-breaking numbers this year and the increased interest in base ball records ~~have~~ has even led to an increase in visitors to the major League baseball hall of fame

Error Summary

Capitalization	9
Language Usage	1
Punctuation:	
Apostrophe	1
Comma	3
Period	2
Quotation Mark	1
Other	2
Spelling	2

WEDNESDAY   **WEEK 12**

adding to the excitement was another record breaking performance this season sammy sosa the powerful batter for the chicago Cubs has been chasing McGwire for the lead in this tight home-run race. With a record 66 home runs he was actually ahead of McGwire before the cardinals' games against the montreal expos this weekend. That's when mcGwire hit the five awesome unforgettable homers that made history

Error Summary

Capitalization	8
Punctuation:	
Apostrophe	1
Comma	4
Period	2
Other	1

THURSDAY   **WEEK 12**

EMC 2728 • Daily Paragraph Editing, Grade 5 • ©2004 by Evan-Moor Corp.

Name _____

when asked about his reaction to this once-in-a-lifetime historic event, McGwire said "to say the least Im amazed. I can't believe I did it can you It blows me away!

McGwire is not the only one whose amazed. fans have been flocking to the ballpark in record=breaking numbers this year and the increased interest in base ball records have even led to an increase in visitors to the major League baseball hall Of fame

WATCH FOR

• quotes
• hyphens

WEDNESDAY   **WEEK 12**

adding to the excitement was another record:breaking performance this season sammy sosa the powerful batter for the chicago Cubs has been chasing McGwire for the lead in this tight home-run race. With a record 66 home runs he was actually ahead of McGwire before the cardinals' games against the montreal expos this weekend. Thats when mcGwire hit the five awesome unforgettable homers that made history

WATCH FOR

• names of sports teams
• commas

THURSDAY   **WEEK 12**

Preview the 4 daily lessons to ensure you review or introduce skills that may be unfamiliar to students.

My Favorite Music

I started listening to popular music when I
was
~~were~~ 11 years old. My dad's mom, Grandma delia,
bought me a boombox for my birthday. I never really
bothered to think about music before, but once I got
a boom box, I started to think about music a lot.
                              listening
after about a month of ~~lissening~~ to a different radio
station every day, I decided that I like listening to
pop, country, rap, and the blues. I have a favorite band
or singer for each type of music.

Error Summary

Capitalization	2
Language Usage	1
Punctuation:	
Comma	7
Period	5
Spelling	2

MONDAY   **WEEK 13**

my favorite pop band is called Three Owls. I
like their song "Hoot Hoot" because it's about a bunch
of kids who like to stay up late. my favorite country
music band, The spurs, has a hit song called "At Dawn"
that is #3 on the music charts. As far as blues songs
go, "Gone Fishing" is my absolute favorite. mom, Dad, and
grandma delia like it, too. If CDs didn't cost so much,
                              copy
we could each have our own ~~copie~~. for now, the four
    have
of us ~~has~~ to share.

Error Summary

Capitalization	7
Language Usage	1
Punctuation:	
Apostrophe	2
Comma	5
Period	3
Quotation Mark	4
Spelling	1

TUESDAY   **WEEK 13**

My Favorite Music

I started listening to popular music when I were 11 years old My dad's mom Grandma delia bought me a boombox for my birthday I never really bothered to think about music before but once I got a boom box, I started to think about music a lot after about a month of lissening to a different radio station every day I decided that I like listening to pop country rap and the blues I have a favorite band or singer for each type of music

• commas

MONDAY   **WEEK 13**

---

my favorite pop band is called Three Owls. I like their song "Hoot Hoot because its about a bunch of kids who like to stay up late. my favorite country music band The spurs, has a hit song called At Dawn that is #3 on the music charts As far as blues songs go Gone Fishing" is my absolute favorite. mom Dad and grandma delia like it, too. If CDs didnt cost so much we could each have our own copie for now, the four of us has to share

• song titles
• apostrophes

TUESDAY   **WEEK 13**

i am the only one in my family who likes rap music grandma delia Mom and dad think rap music

sounds
~~sound~~ like a lot of yelling. I like the way rap songs talk about life For example, Can't Wake Up a song by flip Dillies is about a kid who never makes it to school on time I also like Almost Grown, his song about a teenager who cant wait to grow up. last week, I spent two weeks' worth of allowance to buy the

hottest
~~hotest~~ new CD by big Winnie the famous rap artist

Error Summary

Capitalization	7
Language Usage	1
Punctuation:	
Apostrophe	1
Comma	5
Period	4
Quotation Mark	4
Spelling	1

WEDNESDAY   **WEEK 13**

---

next week is my 13ᵗʰ birthday I made a list of my favorite bands and singers so my family can buy me more CDs our good friend Ramon, who lives next door, drove me down to Music city so I could make sure they had the CDs on my list most of them
were
~~was~~ in stock but a couple were sold out this year, mom said she thinks Im ready for headphones Grandma laughed and said she was just getting used to rap music. grandma rocks!

Error Summary

Capitalization	7
Language Usage	1
Punctuation:	
Apostrophe	1
Comma	1
Period	5

THURSDAY   **WEEK 13**

Name _____

i am the only one in my family who likes rap music grandma delia Mom and dad think rap music sound like a lot of yelling. I like the way rap songs talk about life For example, Can't Wake Up a song by flip Dillies is about a kid who never makes it to school on time I also like Almost Grown, his song about a teenager who cant wait to grow up. last week, I spent two weeks' worth of allowance to buy the hotest new CD by big Winnie the famous rap artist

WATCH FOR

- song titles
- names of singing groups

WEDNESDAY   **WEEK 13**

next week is my 13th birthday I made a list of my favorite bands and singers so my family can buy me more CDs our good friend Ramon, who lives next door, drove me down to Music city so I could make sure they had the CDs on my list most of them was in stock but a couple were sold out this year, mom said she thinks Im ready for headphones Grandma laughed and said she was just getting used to rap music. grandma rocks!

WATCH FOR

- run-on sentences

THURSDAY   **WEEK 13**

Preview the 4 daily lessons to ensure you review or introduce skills that may be unfamiliar to students.

Maui and the Sun

The sun god raced across the sky each day he traveled so fast that people didn't have time to ~~finnish~~ finish their work during the daylight hours. They couldn't grow ~~enuf~~ enough food because there was never enough sunlight to warm the soil and the young growing plants. People were half-starved and ill-tempered.

"Why does the sun god rush?" Maui asked his mother, Hina-of-the-Fire, as she ~~pownded~~ pounded mulberry bark into tapa cloth.

Error Summary	
Capitalization	1
Punctuation:	
Apostrophe	2
Comma	1
Period	2
Quotation Mark	1
Other	1
Spelling	3

MONDAY **WEEK 14**

"The sun has always traveled fast; he always will. That's the way he likes it he always does just what he pleases," said Hina-of-the-Fire, and she breathed a heavy-hearted sigh.

"Then I shall capture the sun god," maui declared boldly "and make him move more slowly. He will be able to enjoy Earth's beauty, and we will enjoy more hours of sunshine."

Error Summary	
Capitalization	2
Punctuation:	
Apostrophe	1
Comma	3
Period	2
Quotation Mark	4
Other	1

TUESDAY **WEEK 14**

Maui and the Sun

The sun god raced across the sky each day he traveled so fast that people didnt have time to finnish their work during the daylight hours. They couldnt grow enuf food because there was never enough sunlight to warm the soil and the young growing plants. People were half-starved and ill tempered.

Why does the sun god rush?" Maui asked his mother, Hina-of-the-Fire as she pownded mulberry bark into tapa cloth

WATCH FOR
- dialog
- spelling

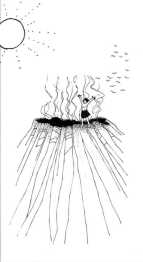

MONDAY   **WEEK 14**

"The sun has always traveled fast; he always will. That's the way he likes it he always does just what he pleases, said Hina-of-the-Fire and she breathed a heavy hearted sigh.

Then I shall capture the sun god, maui declared boldly "and make him move more slowly. He will be able to enjoy Earths beauty and we will enjoy more hours of sunshine

WATCH FOR
- dialog

TUESDAY   **WEEK 14**

"That will not be easy, my son," said Hina-of-the-Fire. "You may need some help."

"I know, Mother, and I know just where I can seek that help," answered maui. "you will see; I shall not fail."

Maui set off for the home of his Grandmother the old one who served the sun god his breakfast ~~brekfast~~ each morning. As his grandmother listened ~~lissened~~ maui explained ~~explain~~ his plan.

Error Summary	
Capitalization	4
Language Usage	1
Punctuation:	
Comma	5
Period	2
Quotation Mark	4
Spelling	2

WEDNESDAY   **WEEK 14**

"Maui, you must ask the Sea Mother for some of her long hair ~~hare~~. you must also gather plant fibers? You shall twist the two ~~too~~ together to make a strong, heavy net" Maui's grandmother explained. "I shall also give you this ax; it has special powers."

"Grandmother, I will do just as you have told ~~tell~~ me. I will make the net as you have said; I will take the ax with it's special powers," maui said confidently as he set off.

Error Summary	
Capitalization	2
Language Usage	1
Punctuation:	
Apostrophe	2
Comma	4
Period	2
Quotation Mark	1
Spelling	2

THURSDAY   **WEEK 14**

"That will not be easy my son, said Hina-of-the-Fire "You may need some help

"I know Mother and I know just where I can seek that help, answered maui. "you will see; I shall not fail.

Maui set off for the home of his Grandmother the old one who served the sun god his brekfast each morning. As his grandmother lissened maui explain his plan.

WATCH FOR

- dialog
- spelling

WEDNESDAY   **WEEK 14**

"Maui you must ask the Sea Mother for some of her long hare. you must also gather plant fibers? You shall twist the too together to make a strong heavy net" Mauis grandmother explained. "I shall also give you this ax; it has special powers"

"Grandmother I will do just as you have tell me. I will make the net as you have said; I will take the ax with it's special powers, maui said confidently as he set off.

WATCH FOR

- dialog
- spelling

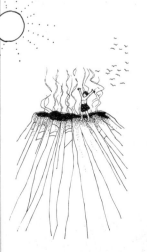

THURSDAY   **WEEK 14**

Preview the 4 daily lessons to ensure you review or introduce skills that may be unfamiliar to students.

The Great Salt Lake

Jim Bridger was a mountain man known for his skill as a trapper trader and guide to wagon trains headed west. In the mid-1820s, Bridger was following the bear river in utah to find where it emptied. When the river came to it's end bridger was standing on a sandy shore looking out at a wide expanse of ~~blew~~ blue water. Gulls circled overhead, and a ~~sent~~ scent of the sea was in the air he scooped up a ~~handfull~~ handful of water and took a sip.

Error Summary

Capitalization	5
Punctuation:	
Apostrophe	1
Comma	3
Period	1
Spelling	3

MONDAY   **WEEK 15**

bridger jumped up in surprise as he spat out the mouthful of water. the water was extremely salty Bridger was amazed. was it possible that the pacific ocean extended so far to the east? As bridger tried to make sense of his confusing discovery he couldnt find ~~no~~ any other explanation. "This must be an inlet of the ocean," he thought. "It must reach much farther inland than anyone ever imagined. It turned out of course, that Bridger was wrong.

Error Summary

Capitalization	6
Language Usage	1
Punctuation:	
Apostrophe	1
Comma	3
Period	2
Quotation Mark	2
Other	1

TUESDAY   **WEEK 15**

EMC 2728 • Daily Paragraph Editing, Grade 5 • ©2004 by Evan-Moor Corp.

Name _____

The Great Salt Lake

Jim Bridger was a mountain man known for his skill as a trapper trader and guide to wagon trains headed west. In the mid-1820s, Bridger was following the bear river in utah to find where it emptied. When the river came to it's end bridger was standing on a sandy shore looking out at a wide expanse of blew water. Gulls circled overhead, and a sent of the sea was in the air he scooped up a handfull of water and took a sip.

- spelling
- names of places

MONDAY   **WEEK 15**

bridger jumped up in surprise as he spat out the mouthful of water. the water was extremely salty Bridger was amazed. was it possible that the pacific ocean extended so far to the east. As bridger tried to make sense of his confusing discovery he couldnt find no other explanation. "This must be an inlet of the ocean, he thought. "It must reach much farther inland than anyone ever imagined. It turned out of course that Bridger was wrong

- quotes
- question marks

TUESDAY   **WEEK 15**

It's no wonder that bridger was confused. As far as he knew only the ocean could be so salty. today, the body of water bridger discovered is fittingly named the Great Salt lake. Besides the river that bridger followed from the north there are three other main rivers that flow into this lake. The weber and ogden rivers enter it from the east the jordan river flows in from the south. There are no rivers however that flow out of the lake

Error Summary

Capitalization	10
Punctuation:	
Apostrophe	1
Comma	4
Period	1
Other	1

WEDNESDAY   **WEEK 15**

The water that flows into the great salt lake contains minerals, including salt. As water evaporates from the lakes surface, these [theese] minerals remain in the lake and give [gives] the water it's high salt content. About two million tons of dissolved salt enters the lake each year in this manner In the mid-1800s, people began to extract salt from the lake for commercial use. to this day, companies continue [continu] to collect salt from the great Salt lake.

Error Summary

Capitalization	6
Language Usage	1
Punctuation:	
Apostrophe	2
Comma	1
Period	1
Spelling	2

THURSDAY   **WEEK 15**

Name ⎯⎯⎯⎯⎯⎯⎯⎯⎯⎯⎯⎯⎯⎯⎯⎯⎯⎯⎯⎯⎯⎯

Its no wonder that bridger was confused. As far as he knew only the ocean could be so salty. today, the body of water bridger discovered is fittingly named the Great Salt lake. Besides the river that bridger followed from the north there are three other main rivers that flow into this lake. The weber and ogden rivers enter it from the east the jordan river flows in from the south. There are no rivers however that flow out of the lake

WATCH FOR

• semicolon

WEDNESDAY   **WEEK 15**

The water that flows into the great salt lake contains minerals, including salt. As water evaporates from the lakes surface theese minerals remain in the lake and gives the water it's high salt content. About two million tons of dissolved salt enters the lake each year in this manner In the mid-1800s, people began to extract salt from the lake for commercial use. to this day, companies continu to collect salt from the great Salt lake.

WATCH FOR

• apostrophes
• names of places

THURSDAY   **WEEK 15**

Preview the 4 daily lessons to ensure you review or introduce skills that may be unfamiliar to students.

Colonial Holidays

november 27, 1726

Dear Diary,

This is our second thanksgiving in Boston. Mama, keri nellie and I ~~has~~ *have* been cooking for two days. Nellie and I are in charge of shelling the clams and mussels for the shellfish chowder. keri is shucking the corn and shelling lima beans for succotash. Mama, of course, is baking ~~his~~ *her* delicious ~~pumkin~~ *pumpkin* pie.

Error Summary	
Capitalization	5
Language Usage	2
Punctuation:	
Comma	6
Period	3
Spelling	1

MONDAY   **WEEK 16**

december 24, 1726

dear ~~Dairy~~ *Diary*,

The whole family ~~are~~ *is* working hard in preparation for our christmas festivities. Papa has decorated all of ~~hour~~ *our* windows with evergreen branches. meanwhile keri nellie and I have been stringing cranberries. Mama and mrs Helik our next-door ~~neihbor~~ *neighbor* are preparing our christmas feast.

Error Summary	
Capitalization	8
Language Usage	1
Punctuation:	
Comma	6
Period	4
Other	1
Spelling	3

TUESDAY   **WEEK 16**

Colonial Holidays

WATCH FOR

- commas

november 27: 1726

Dear Diary

    This is our second thanksgiving in Boston. Mama keri nellie and I has been cooking for two days Nellie and I are in charge of shelling the clams and mussels for the shellfish chowder keri is shucking the corn and shelling lima beans for succotash. Mama, of course is baking his delicious pumkin pie

MONDAY   **WEEK 16**

december 24. 1726

WATCH FOR

- names of holidays
- hyphens

dear Dairy,

    The whole family are working hard in preparation for our christmas festivities Papa has decorated all of hour windows with evergreen branches meanwhile keri nellie and I have been stringing cranberries. Mama and mrs Helik our next door neihbor are preparing our christmas feast

TUESDAY   **WEEK 16**

january 5, 1727

Dear diary,

Twelfth night my favorite holiday are tomorrow.
All the grown-ups put on their best clothes and dance
to merry music This year, mama papa and keri my
older sister is going to the twelfth night ball. I am
too young to go Keri promised to tell me everything.
I can hardly wait to grow up but I know I must

Error Summary

Capitalization	9
Language Usage	2
Punctuation:	
Comma	8
Period	3
Other	1

WEDNESDAY   **WEEK 16**

April 19, 1727

dear Diary,

I have spent days hunting for the biggest eggs
I can find. I only have seven but easter is tomorrow
so that will have to do. Nellie my younger sister made
dye for the eggs she used tree bark onion skins beet
juice and spinach water. keri are cutting out patterns.
I, meanwhile am waiting to dye the eggs

Error Summary

Capitalization	4
Language Usage	1
Punctuation:	
Comma	10
Period	2

THURSDAY   **WEEK 16**

EMC 2728 • Daily Paragraph Editing, Grade 5 • ©2004 by Evan-Moor Corp.

january 5, 1727

WATCH FOR

Dear diary;

- commas
- verb tenses

    Twelfth night my favorite holiday are tomorrow. All the grown=ups put on their best clothes and dance to merry music This year, mama papa and keri my older sister is going to the twelfth night ball. I am too young to go Keri promised to tell me everything. I can hardly wait to grow up but I know I must

---

WEDNESDAY   **WEEK 16**

April 19; 1727

WATCH FOR

dear Diary.

- commas

    I have spent days hunting for the biggest eggs I can find. I only have seven but easter is tomorrow so that will have to do. Nellie my younger sister made dye for the eggs she used tree bark onion skins beet juice and spinach water. keri are cutting out patterns. I, meanwhile am waiting to dye the eggs

THURSDAY   **WEEK 16**

Preview the 4 daily lessons to ensure you review or introduce skills that may be unfamiliar to students.

The Battle at Little Big Horn

Over 125 years ago a battle was fought at the Little big horn a valley in montana. On june 25 1876 the troops of the United states Armys seventh cavalry clashed with warriors of the sioux and cheyenne Nations. By the time the sun went down that day the US Army had suffered the worst defeat in it's history and a popular Civil war hero was dead. Lieutenant Colonel george armstrong Custer had made his now-famous "last stand.

Error Summary	
Capitalization	12
Punctuation:	
Apostrophe	2
Comma	6
Period	2
Quotation Mark	1

MONDAY   **WEEK 17**

Lt Col custer had risen quickly through the ranks of the u.s Army and had ~~prove~~ *proven* his daring and courage during bloody civil War battles, including the famous battle at gettysburg. When the civil war ended custer remained in the army and was put in command of the seventh cavalry. it was as the leader of this force that custer was sent to fight against the Plains Indian tribes, who knew him by the nickname "Long Hair."

Error Summary	
Capitalization	12
Language Usage	1
Punctuation:	
Comma	1
Period	4
Quotation Mark	1

TUESDAY   **WEEK 17**

Name —————————————————————————————

The Battle at Little Big Horn

Over 125 years ago a battle was fought at the Little big horn a valley in montana. On june 25 1876 the troops of the United states Armys seventh cavalry clashed with warriors of the sioux and cheyenne Nations. By the time the sun went down that day the US Army had suffered the worst defeat in it's history and a popular Civil war hero was dead. Lieutenant Colonel george armstrong Custer had made his now-famous "last stand.

WATCH FOR

- names of groups of people
- abbreviations

MONDAY   **WEEK 17**

Lt Col custer had risen quickly through the ranks of the u.s Army and had prove his daring and courage during bloody civil War battles, including the famous battle at gettysburg. When the civil war ended custer remained in the army and was put in command of the seventh cavalry. it was as the leader of this force that custer was sent to fight against the Plains Indian tribes, who knew him by the nickname Long Hair"

WATCH FOR

- names of people
- names of places
- names of events
- abbreviations

TUESDAY   **WEEK 17**

As white intruders continued to break treaty

agreements

~~agrements~~ and move onto sacred lands in montanas

Black hills Native american warriors gathered to fight

their

for ~~there~~ land. Custers' cavalry troops had been

active in battles against the Indians through out the

spring of 1876. in the early summer custer was asked

defeat

to lead his troops on a mission to find and ~~defeet~~

the sioux and cheyenne warriors who were defending

their lands

WEDNESDAY   **WEEK 17**

When Custers scouts spotted an indian camp

along the rosebud river in the valley of the Little

big horn Custer made a series of mistakes that

cost him and his troops their lives. First, custer

split his forces into three groups. He also seriously

underestimated the number of indian warriors in the

camp. When custer led his forces in to attack they

were quickly outnumbered and encircled on an open

plain

~~plane~~. Within just an hour all were dead.

THURSDAY   **WEEK 17**

Name _____

As white intruders continued to break treaty agrements and move onto sacred lands in montanas Black hills Native american warriors gathered to fight for there land. Custers' cavalry troops had been active in battles against the Indians through out the spring of 1876. in the early summer custer was asked to lead his troops on a mission to find and defeet the sioux and cheyenne warriors who were defending their lands

- spelling
- apostrophes

WEDNESDAY   **WEEK 17**

When Custers scouts spotted an indian camp along the rosebud river in the valley of the Little big horn Custer made a series of mistakes that cost him and his troops their lives. First, custer split his forces into three groups. He also seriously underestimated the number of indian warriors in the camp. When custer led his forces in to attack they were quickly outnumbered and encircled on an open plane. Within just an hour all were dead.

- names of people
- names of places

THURSDAY   **WEEK 17**

Preview the 4 daily lessons to ensure you review or introduce skills that may be unfamiliar to students.

Golden Gate Bridge

The Golden Gate Bridge stands high above the choppy cold water of the San Francisco Bay. To the northwest stands mt. tamalpais with its groves of ancient ~~antient~~ redwood trees that stand over 60 meters (200 ft.) tall. to the east, the rugged dry hills are covered with brush oak trees and wheat colored grass. Behind the southern entrance of the ~~brigde~~ bridge, san Francisco's high rises stand tall, the backdrop of the busy city

Error Summary	
Capitalization	4
Punctuation:	
Comma	4
Period	1
Other	2
Spelling	2

MONDAY   **WEEK 18**

---

the golden gate bridge is one of the worlds most beautiful bridges. The bridge looks red It is not red however or even golden it is, in fact a color called "international orange It is an amazing ~~struture~~ structure. It is the gateway that connects the northern and southern shores of san francisco Bay The bridge has two massive towers that reach 227 meters (746 ft) into the air. the platform of the bridge runs about 1 mile ~~acros~~ across the bay and is 67 meters (220 ft) above the water

Error Summary	
Capitalization	8
Punctuation:	
Apostrophe	1
Comma	3
Period	7
Quotation Mark	1
Spelling	2

TUESDAY   **WEEK 18**

EMC 2728 • Daily Paragraph Editing, Grade 5 • ©2004 by Evan-Moor Corp.

Golden Gate Bridge

The Golden Gate Bridge stands high above the choppy cold water of the San Francisco Bay. To the northwest stands mt. tamalpais with its groves of antient redwood trees that stand over 60 meters (200 ft.) tall. to the east, the rugged dry hills are covered with brush oak trees and wheat/colored grass. Behind the southern entrance of the brigde, san Francisco's high=rises stand tall, the backdrop of the busy city

- commas
- hyphens

MONDAY   **WEEK 18**

---

the golden gate bridge is one of the worlds most beautiful bridges. The bridge looks red It is not red however or even golden it is, in fact a color called "international orange It is an amazing struture. It is the gateway that connects the northern and southern shores of san francisco Bay The bridge has two massive towers that reach 227 meters (746 ft) into the air. the platform of the bridge runs about 1 mile acros the bay and is 67 meters (220 ft) above the water

- abbreviations
- spelling

TUESDAY   **WEEK 18**

two steel cables run the length of the bridge
They sweep to the top of the first set of towers
where they are anchored they then slope downward,
reaching their lowest point in the middle of the
bridge the ~~cabels~~ *cables* then climb to the second set of
towers they hang like a pair of jump ropes suspended
between the two towers. vertical ~~steal~~ *steel* cables run
from the bridge platform and attach to the sloping
cables overhead. The platform is suspended, or hung
from the cables This is why the golden gate is called
a suspension bridge

Error Summary	
Capitalization	7
Punctuation:	
Comma	1
Period	6
Spelling	2

WEDNESDAY   **WEEK 18**

The golden Gate bridge has served as both a
pedestrian and a vehicular crossing for more than
a half-century. Its original purpose was to provide
an economical high-speed transportation link between
the city of san Francisco and the County of marin
In addition to accomplishing this goal, the bridge has
~~became~~ *become* the symbol of san Francisco. in fact, this
spectacular structure is world-renowned. it is one of
the most visited sites in the world

Error Summary	
Capitalization	8
Language Usage	1
Punctuation:	
Comma	2
Period	2
Other	3

THURSDAY   **WEEK 18**

EMC 2728 • Daily Paragraph Editing, Grade 5 • ©2004 by Evan-Moor Corp.

Name _____

two steel cables run the length of the bridge They sweep to the top of the first set of towers where they are anchored they then slope downward, reaching their lowest point in the middle of the bridge the cabels then climb to the second set of towers they hang like a pair of jump ropes suspended between the two towers. vertical steal cables run from the bridge platform and attach to the sloping cables overhead. The platform is suspended, or hung from the cables This is why the golden gate is called a suspension bridge

- run-on sentences

WEDNESDAY	WEEK 18

The golden Gate bridge has served as both a pedestrian and a vehicular crossing for more than a half=century. Its original purpose was to provide an economical high>speed transportation link between the city of san Francisco and the County of marin In addition to accomplishing this goal the bridge has became the symbol of san Francisco. in fact this spectacular structure is world/renowned. it is one of the most visited sites in the world

- hyphens

THURSDAY	WEEK 18

Preview the 4 daily lessons to ensure you review or introduce skills that may be unfamiliar to students.

Jane Goodall's Wild Life

Jane goodall was born on april 3, 1934, in London, england. She grewed [grew] up on englands sunny southern Coast in the seaside town of bournemouth. The town is known for its seven mile stretch of lovely uninterrupted beaches. Nearby is New Forest where wild ponies rome [roam] freely. With such wonderful surroundings, its no surprise that Jane loved nature; nor is it a surprise that she expressed interest in becoming a scientist at an early age.

Error Summary

Capitalization	6
Language Usage	1
Punctuation:	
Apostrophe	2
Comma	6
Period	1
Other	1
Spelling	1

MONDAY   **WEEK 19**

As a young girl, jane loved to read about african animals, and she especially enjoyed rudyard Kiplings *Just So Stories*. She also enjoyed writing, and her mother helped her produce her own weekly newspaper about animals. When Jane finished school, her mother could not afford to send her to the university, so jane began working. after several years, a school friend invited Jane to visit her in kenya, so Janes dream of seeing africa came true.

Error Summary

Capitalization	7
Punctuation:	
Apostrophe	2
Comma	5
Period	1
Other	1

TUESDAY   **WEEK 19**

Jane Goodall's Wild Life

Jane goodall was born on april 3 1934 in London england. She growed up on englands sunny southern Coast in the seaside town of bournemouth. The town is known for its seven_mile stretch of lovely uninterrupted beaches. Nearby is New Forest where wild ponies rome freely. With such wonderful surroundings its no surprise that Jane loved nature; nor is it a surprise that she expressed interest in becoming a scientist at an early age

- names of places
- commas

MONDAY   **WEEK 19**

As a young girl, jane loved to read about african animals and she especially enjoyed rudyard Kiplings Just So Stories. She also enjoyed writing and her mother helped her produce her own weekly newspaper about animals. When Jane finished school her mother could not afford to send her to the university so jane began working. after several years, a school friend invited Jane to visit her in kenya so Janes dream of seeing africa came true

- book titles
- names of places

TUESDAY   **WEEK 19**

It was in 1957 at the age of 23 that Jane arrived in kenya. After visiting her friend, Jane hoped to stay on in africa to study. She went to see Dr. louis leakey a famous scientist who was studying the earliest history of humankind through fossils and bones found in africa. After Jane had worked for a time with dr leakey he suggested that she study the chimpanzees near lake tanganyika in Tanzania this was a life-changing move for Jane.

Error Summary

Capitalization	10
Language Usage	1
Punctuation:	
Comma	3
Period	3
Other	1
Spelling	2

WEDNESDAY **WEEK 19**

Jane spent winters in england at cambridge University but she spent the rest of her time with the chimps she observed their behavior and made many discoveries, including new ways to study animal communities. Jane has written many books, including "My life with the chimpanzees." She has also been the subject of numerous books, such as the childrens book Jane Goodall: pioneer Researcher by jayne pettit read it to learn more about her.

Error Summary

Capitalization	9
Punctuation:	
Apostrophe	1
Comma	1
Period	2
Quotation Mark	2
Other	2

THURSDAY **WEEK 19**

It was in 1957 at the age of 23 that Jane arrived in kenya. After visiting her friend Jane hope to stay on in africa to study. She went to see Dr louis leakey a famous sientist who was studying the earlyest history of humankind through fossils and bones found in africa. After Jane had worked for a time with dr leakey he suggested that she study the chimpanzees near lake tanganyika in Tanzania this was a life=changing move for Jane.

- abbreviations
- names of places

WEDNESDAY   **WEEK 19**

Jane spent winters in england at cambridge University but she spent the rest of her time with the chimps she observed their behavior and made many discoveries, including new ways to study animal communities. Jane has written many books, including "My life with the chimpanzees." She has also been the subject of numerous books, such as the childrens book Jane Goodall: pioneer Researcher by jayne pettit read it to learn more about her.

- book titles

THURSDAY   **WEEK 19**

Preview the 4 daily lessons to ensure you review or introduce skills that may be unfamiliar to students.

Year-Round School

schools across america are looking at ways to improve education One option is to implement a year-round academic calendar A year-round calendar schedules several breaks throughout the school year and three weeks of vacation during the summer months traditionally, american schools have operated on a ten-month system, which schedules two full months of summer vacation, as well as other holiday breaks

Error Summary

Capitalization	4
Punctuation:	
Period	4
Other	1

MONDAY   **WEEK 20**

---

although figuring out the best possible vacation schedule is a top priority for most students, administrators have a more challenging task they need to evaluate ~~weather~~ whether a year-round education improves student achievement advocates of year-round schooling believe that shorter summer vacations may increase students' retention of knowledge as a result teachers will spend less time reviewing the previous year's curriculum

Error Summary

Capitalization	4
Punctuation:	
Apostrophe	2
Comma	2
Period	4
Other	1
Spelling	1

TUESDAY   **WEEK 20**

Year-Round School

schools across america are looking at ways to improve education One option is to implement a year-round academic calendar A year:round calendar schedules several breaks throughout the school year and three weeks of vacation during the summer months traditionally, american schools have operated on a ten-month system, which schedules two full months of summer vacation, as well as other holiday breaks

• hyphens

MONDAY   **WEEK 20**

although figuring out the best possible vacation schedule is a top priority for most students administrators have a more challenging task they need to evaluate weather a year-round education improves student achievement advocates of year=round schooling believe that shorter summer vacations may increase students retention of knowledge as a result teachers will spend less time reviewing the previous years curriculum

• run-on sentences
• apostrophes

TUESDAY   **WEEK 20**

students in year-round and ten-month programs spend 180 days in the classroom However, with less time spent on review teachers are able to cover more material throughout the year this means that students who attend year-round schools may have the opportunity to learn more than students in the traditional ten-month system this is only one of the benefits of year-round school

Error Summary

Capitalization	3
Punctuation:	
Comma	1
Period	4
Other	4

WEDNESDAY   **WEEK 20**

a year-round calendar can help solve the problem of overcrowded schools by using a system called "multiple-track education this system creates a staggered schedule that allows schools to increase their enrollment by one-third. multi-track scheduling rotates school breaks among several groups of students; one-third of the student body is always on break Year-round school is a sensible solution to the problem of overcrowded schools

Error Summary

Capitalization	3
Punctuation:	
Period	3
Quotation Mark	1
Other	5

THURSDAY   **WEEK 20**

EMC 2728 • Daily Paragraph Editing, Grade 5 • ©2004 by Evan-Moor Corp.

Name _____

• hyphens

students in year=round and ten-month programs spend 180 days in the classroom However, with less time spent on review teachers are able to cover more material throughout the year this means that students who attend year:round schools may have the opportunity to learn more than students in the traditional ten=month system this is only one of the benefits of year^round school

WEDNESDAY   **WEEK 20**

• hyphens
• special words in quotes

a year=round calendar can help solve the problem of overcrowded schools by using a system called "multiple-track education this system creates a staggered schedule that allows schools to increase their enrollment by one third. multi:track scheduling rotates school breaks among several groups of students; one=third of the student body is always on break Year:round school is a sensible solution to the problem of overcrowded schools

THURSDAY   **WEEK 20**

Preview the 4 daily lessons to ensure you review or introduce skills that may be unfamiliar to students.

Mr. Brady's Photography Studio

It has now been two months since I began working in matthew brady's photography studio The studio is long narrow and crowded with supplies However at the rear of the studio is a small room that I call home I awaken daily at 5:00 a.m. to prepare mr brady's photography supplies. I must wipe down the silver box and prepare the iodine for the photograph or "daguerreotype," which is what they call this amazing way of capturing an image

Error Summary

Capitalization	4
Punctuation:	
Comma	4
Period	5
Quotation Mark	1

MONDAY   **WEEK 21**

although I have little experience working with such complex equipment Mr Brady has allowed me to work as his apprentice I met him on my long journey from ohio to new york city the train was crowded and he asked me if he could store his equipment in my overhead compartment. As I had only a few items I obliged. when I inquired about his odd-looking boxes, I learned that he was matthew brady the well-known photographer

Error Summary

Capitalization	9
Punctuation:	
Comma	5
Period	4
Other	2

TUESDAY   **WEEK 21**

Name —————————————————————————

Mr. Brady's Photography Studio

It has now been two months since I began working in matthew brady's photography studio The studio is long narrow and crowded with supplies However at the rear of the studio is a small room that I call home I awaken daily at 5:00 a.m. to prepare mr brady's photography supplies. I must wipe down the silver box and prepare the iodine for the photograph or daguerreotype," which is what they call this amazing way of capturing an image

- special words in quotes

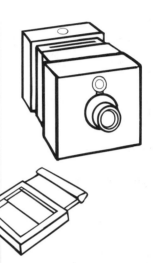

MONDAY	**WEEK 21**

although I have little experience working with such complex equipment Mr Brady has allowed me to work as his apprentice I met him on my long journey from ohio to new york city the train was crowded and he asked me if he could store his equipment in my overhead compartment. As I had only a few items I obliged. when I inquired about his odd=looking boxes I learned that he was matthew brady the well:known photographer

- names of people
- names of places
- hyphens

TUESDAY	**WEEK 21**

By the time we arrived in new york city Mr brady had agreed to take me on as his apprentice in exchange for lodging this has been a life-changing experience for me. Since I have been in new york I have seen many of the well-known subjects who have "sat for ~~portriats~~ portraits by mr brady. perhaps most exciting for me was to see abe lincoln our beloved president who was photographed both alone and with his family.

Error Summary	
Capitalization	12
Punctuation:	
Comma	4
Period	3
Quotation Mark	1
Other	2
Spelling	1

WEDNESDAY　　　　　　　　　**WEEK 21**

i have gained much experience in handling the photography equipment Many hours of work in what mr. Brady calls the "dark room" have been invaluable to me I have gained knowledge of how to use mercury and how to apply salt solution to create a clear image I never imagined that traveling to New york would acquaint me with such a profession and with such prominent people It seems I am living an incredible, unbelievable dream yet it's real!

Error Summary	
Capitalization	3
Punctuation:	
Apostrophe	1
Comma	2
Period	4
Quotation Mark	1
Other	1

THURSDAY　　　　　　　　　**WEEK 21**

EMC 2728 • Daily Paragraph Editing, Grade 5 • ©2004 by Evan-Moor Corp.

Name _____

By the time we arrived in new york city Mr brady had agreed to take me on as his apprentice in exchange for lodging this has been a life+changing experience for me. Since I have been in new york I have seen many of the well>known subjects who have "sat for portriats by mr brady. perhaps most exciting for me was to see abe lincoln our beloved president who was photographed both alone and with his family.

WATCH FOR

- hyphens
- abbreviations

WEDNESDAY   **WEEK 21**

i have gained much experience in handling the photography equipment Many hours of work in what mr. Brady calls the dark room" have been invaluable to me I have gained knowledge of how to use mercury and how to apply salt solution to create a clear image I never imagined that traveling to New york would acquaint me with such a profession and with such prominent people It seems I am living an incredible unbelievable dream yet its real

WATCH FOR

- special words in quotes

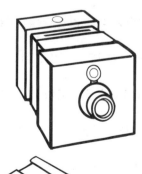

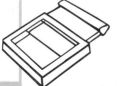

THURSDAY   **WEEK 21**

Preview the 4 daily lessons to ensure you review or introduce skills that may be unfamiliar to students.

Space Science Is Far-Out!

NASA's Ames Aerospace Encounter is a daylong program created for fourth-, fifth-, and sixth-grade students. this interactive program is held in a unique classroom setting where NASA turns learning about science, mathematics, and technology into an out-of-this-world experience. Class is held in a renovated supersonic wind tunnel. subjects include Space Sciences, Aeronautics, Space Station Physics, and Earth Science.

Error Summary	
Capitalization	2
Punctuation:	
Comma	8
Period	4

MONDAY   **WEEK 22**

students spend thirty minutes learning about each subject. they get physical in their Space Sciences class while learning the basics of physics. ~~Principals~~ Principles of flight, wind tunnels, and airplane design are three of the topics covered in Aeronautics. in Space Station Physics, students become astronauts on a simulated space mission. they complete several experiments during the out-of-this-world simulation. the last lesson covers Earth Science concepts.

Error Summary	
Capitalization	5
Punctuation:	
Comma	3
Period	3
Other	3
Spelling	1

TUESDAY   **WEEK 22**

Space Science Is Far-Out!

NASA's Ames Aerospace Encounter is a daylong program created for fourth- fifth- and sixth-grade students this interactive program is held in a unique classroom setting where NASA turns learning about science mathematics and technology into an out-of-this-world experience Class is held in a renovated supersonic wind tunnel subjects include Space Sciences Aeronautics Space Station Physics and Earth Science

- commas
- run-on sentences

MONDAY   **WEEK 22**

students spend thirty minutes learning about each subject they get physical in their Space Sciences class while learning the basics of physics. Principals of flight wind tunnels and airplane design are three of the topics covered in Aeronautics. in Space Station Physics students become astronauts on a simulated space mission they complete several experiments during the out of this world simulation. the last lesson covers Earth Science concepts

- hyphens
- run-on sentences

TUESDAY   **WEEK 22**

the aerospace Encounter program offers students a once-in-a-lifetime opportunity to immerse themselves in science and explore the possibilities of our future in space. instead of limiting students' learning to books NASA provides students with a hands-on learning experience. These real-life experiences give students a strong foundation to build on and connect well with current science programs.

Error Summary	
Capitalization	3
Punctuation:	
Apostrophe	1
Comma	1
Period	1
Other	3

WEDNESDAY   **WEEK 22**

The ames aerospace encounter program is an exciting way to spark student ~~intrest~~ interest in becoming the deep space pioneers of the future. NASA has ~~suceeded~~ succeeded in combining learning with the thrill of hands-on experience. with a supersonic wind tunnel for a classroom, an astronaut for a teacher, and space sciences as the subject, NASA has created an unforgettable learning experience.

Error Summary	
Capitalization	6
Punctuation:	
Comma	3
Period	1
Other	2
Spelling	2

THURSDAY   **WEEK 22**

the aerospace Encounter program offers students a once=in a-lifetime opportunity to immerse themselves in science and explore the possibilities of our future in space. instead of limiting students learning to books NASA provides students with a hands-on learning experience These real life experiences give students a strong foundation to build on and connect well with current science programs.

WATCH FOR

• hyphens

WEDNESDAY   **WEEK 22**

The ames aerospace encounter program is an exciting way to spark student intrest in becoming the deep:space pioneers of the future. NASA has suceeded in combining learning with the thrill of hands=on experience. with a supersonic wind tunnel for a classroom an astronaut for a teacher and space sciences as the subject NASA has created an unforgettable learning experience

WATCH FOR

• hyphens
• spelling

THURSDAY   **WEEK 22**

Preview the 4 daily lessons to ensure you review or introduce skills that may be unfamiliar to students.

The Power of Magnets

h̲ave you ever wondered why magnets are able to push or pull certain objects? ᴀ magnet is made from steel or mixtures of iron and other metals. Magnets attract, or pull, other "magnetic" metals. i̲ron, steel, cobalt, and nickel are magnetic. d̲oes this mean that if a large magnet were placed above a steel car, it would attract it? Youv̌e got it! j̲unkyards use powerful electromagnets to move heavy metal objects from place to place.

Error Summary

Capitalization	5
Punctuation:	
Apostrophe	1
Comma	3
Period	1
Other	2

MONDAY　　　　　**WEEK 23**

Magnets have two poles, or ends. The north-seeking pole always ~~try~~ *tries* to point toward magnetic north. The south–seeking pole tries to point south. If you put the north pole of one magnet near the south pole of another magnet, you can feel the magnets attract, or pull, on each other. But if you put two poles of the same kind ~~togeather~~ *together* they will repel, or push away, each other. ~~Their~~ *There* is a rule to help you remember this. The rule is "Like poles repel, unlike poles attract."

Error Summary

Language Usage	1
Punctuation:	
Comma	6
Quotation Mark	1
Other	1
Spelling	2

TUESDAY　　　　　**WEEK 23**

The Power of Magnets

• question marks

have you ever wondered why magnets are able to push or pull certain objects a magnet is made from steel or mixtures of iron and other metals. Magnets attract, or pull, other "magnetic" metals. iron steel cobalt and nickel are magnetic. does this mean that if a large magnet were placed above a steel car, it would attract it Youve got it! junkyards use powerful electromagnets to move heavy metal objects from place to place,

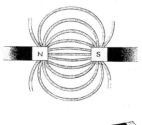

MONDAY   **WEEK 23**

• commas
• spelling

Magnets have two poles, or ends. The north-seeking pole always try to point toward magnetic north. The south seeking pole tries to point south. If you put the north pole of one magnet near the south pole of another magnet you can feel the magnets attract or pull on each other. But if you put two poles of the same kind togeather they will repel or push away each other. Their is a rule to help you remember this. The rule is "Like poles repel, unlike poles attract.

TUESDAY   **WEEK 23**

around AD 1600 william gilbert an english physician discovered that Earth has a magnetic field. when Gilbert used lodestone to make a simple compass he realized that Earths magnetic field caused the compass needle to swing north before Gilberts discovery people *believed* that a star in the big dipper or iron-capped mountains in the north attracted compass needles

Error Summary	
Capitalization	8
Punctuation:	
Apostrophe	2
Comma	5
Period	4
Other	1
Spelling	1

WEDNESDAY   **WEEK 23**

Magnets have many *important* uses all electric motors use magnets. these motors run *refrigerators* CD players sanders and electric toys doctors also use magnets in *their* work. They use a procedure called Magnetic Resonance Imaging (MRI) to see images of their patients head spine and other body parts. science continues to find new *ways* to use the power of magnets

Error Summary	
Capitalization	4
Punctuation:	
Apostrophe	1
Comma	5
Period	3
Spelling	4

THURSDAY   **WEEK 23**

EMC 2728 • Daily Paragraph Editing, Grade 5 • ©2004 by Evan-Moor Corp.

around AD 1600 william gilbert an english physician discovered that Earth has a magnetic field. when Gilbert used lodestone to make a simple compass he realized that Earths magnetic field caused the compass needle to swing north before Gilberts discovery people beleived that a star in the big dipper or iron=capped mountains in the north attracted compass needles

- names of constellations
- hyphens

WEDNESDAY   **WEEK 23**

Magnets have many importent uses all electric motors use magnets. these motors run refrigertators CD players sanders and electric toys doctors also use magnets in there work. They use a procedure called Magnetic Resonance Imaging (MRI) to see images of their patients head spine and other body parts. science continues to find new waes to use the power of magnets

- run-on sentences
- spelling

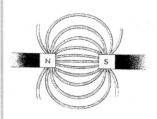

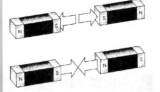

THURSDAY   **WEEK 23**

Preview the 4 daily lessons to ensure you review or introduce skills that may be unfamiliar to students.

An Extreme Continent

The continent of antarctica is a land of extremes it is located farther south than any of the other six continents and includes the geographic South Pole Although 98% of Antarctica is covered with ice this icy continent actually boasts the worlds larger dessert. That's because a desert is defined as an area that receives less than 254 millimeters (10 in.) of rain or precipitation each year Antarctica receives only about 50 millimeters (2 in) each year

largest *desert*

Error Summary

Capitalization	2
Language Usage	1
Punctuation:	
Apostrophe	2
Comma	1
Period	5
Spelling	1

MONDAY   **WEEK 24**

the coldest temperature ever recorded on Earth was measured on antarctica; it was ⁻128.6° Fahrenheit. It's no surprise therefore that the ground on this continent is frozen. Very little moisture evaporates in antarctica so the snow that falls stays on the ground Over time, it has built up into a massive sheet of ice that covers most of the continent the rest of the continent about 2% is rock

ground

built

Error Summary

Capitalization	4
Language Usage	1
Punctuation:	
Apostrophe	1
Comma	5
Period	3
Spelling	1

TUESDAY   **WEEK 24**

EMC 2728 • Daily Paragraph Editing, Grade 5 • ©2004 by Evan-Moor Corp.

Name _____

An Extreme Continent

The continent of antarctica is a land of extremes it is located farther south than any of the other six continents and includes the geographic South Pole Although 98% of Antarctica is covered with ice this icy continent actually boasts the worlds larger dessert. Thats because a desert is defined as an area that receives less than 254 millimeters (10 in.) of rain or precipitation each year Antarctica receives only about 50 millimeters (2 in) each year

- apostrophes
- abbreviations

MONDAY   **WEEK 24**

the coldest temperature ever recorded on Earth was measured on antarctica; it was ⁻128.6° Fahrenheit. Its no surprise therefore that the grownd on this continent is frozen. Very little moisture evaporates in antarctica so the snow that falls stays on the ground Over time, it has build up into a massive sheet of ice that covers most of the continent the rest of the continent about 2% is rock

- commas
- verb tenses

TUESDAY   **WEEK 24**

although it may seem hard to believe antarctica was not always located over the South pole. Scientists believe that ~~antartica~~ Antarctica was located near Earth's equator about 500 million years ago the continents climate was very different than it is today so life on the continent was also very different. Dinosaur ~~fosills~~ fossils found in antarctica show how dramatically the continent has changed?

Error Summary

Capitalization	6
Punctuation:	
Apostrophe	1
Comma	2
Period	2
Spelling	2

WEDNESDAY   **WEEK 24**

today however there ~~is~~ are no trees or bushes on Antarctica. Plant life is limited to mosses lichens and algae. most of the regions larger animals such as penguins and ~~seels~~ seals spend most of ~~there~~ their time in the waters around the frozen continent. Mites ticks and worms are among Antarctica's most common land animals There ~~aren't~~ are no permanent human residents on the continent, although scientists spend time at research bases

Error Summary

Capitalization	2
Language Usage	2
Punctuation:	
Apostrophe	2
Comma	8
Period	2
Spelling	2

THURSDAY   **WEEK 24**

EMC 2728 • Daily Paragraph Editing, Grade 5 • ©2004 by Evan-Moor Corp.

although it may seem hard to believe antarctica was not always located over the South pole. Scientists believe that antartica was located near Earth's equator about 500 million years ago the continents climate was very different than it is today so life on the continent was also very different. Dinosaur fosills found in antarctica show how dramatically the continent has changed?

- apostrophes
- spelling

WEDNESDAY   **WEEK 24**

today however there is no trees or bushes on Antarctica. Plant life is limited to mosses lichens and algae. most of the regions larger animals such as penguins and seels spend most of there time in the waters around the frozen continent. Mites ticks and worms are among Antarcticas most common land animals There aren't no permanent human residents on the continent, although scientists spend time at research bases

- commas
- apostrophes

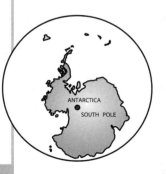

ANTARCTICA

SOUTH POLE

THURSDAY   **WEEK 24**

Preview the 4 daily lessons to ensure you review or introduce skills that may be unfamiliar to students.

Vacation Letters

Powder ridge lodge

january, 3, 2004

dear morgan,

   Happy new year buddy! I still can't ~~beleive~~ believe you ~~gotten~~ got the stomach flu the day before our ~~anual~~ annual ski trip. We've really missed you and we've all been hoping that ~~your~~ you're feeling a lot better. By the time you get this well be enjoying the snow.

Error Summary

Capitalization	7
Language Usage	1
Punctuation:	
Apostrophe	2
Comma	4
Spelling	3

MONDAY   **WEEK 25**

   You can't believe how much snow has fallen since christmas! We wake up every ~~mourning~~ morning to find the mountains covered with a fresh, pure layer of white powder. all the snow has made for some great snowboarding and skiing. It's ~~to~~ too bad you couldn't be here, but we'll count on you for next winter.

   your friend,
   Nick

Error Summary

Capitalization	3
Punctuation:	
Comma	2
Period	1
Spelling	2

TUESDAY   **WEEK 25**

Name _____

Vacation Letters

Powder ridge lodge

january, 3, 2004

dear morgan,

Happy new year buddy! I still can't beleive you gotten the stomach flu the day before our anual ski trip. Weve really missed you and we've all been hoping that your feeling a lot better. By the time you get this well be enjoying the snow.

MONDAY   **WEEK 25**

You can't believe how much snow has fallen since christmas! We wake up every mourning to find the mountains covered with a fresh pure layer of white powder. all the snow has made for some great snowboarding and skiing. It's to bad you couldn't be here, but we'll count on you for next winter

your friend

Nick

TUESDAY   **WEEK 25**

---

orlando Florida
January 5 2004

dear Nick

I know you're not going to believe me but I promise you that I'm tell *telling* you the truth! i'm here in florida spending a few days with my cousins. My mom and I flew here on january 2nd and I'll be home the day before school starts

Error Summary

Capitalization	5
Language Usage	1
Punctuation:	
Comma	5
Period	1

WEDNESDAY   **WEEK 25**

Mom had to go to a conference in orlando for her job. of course I was supposed to be gone on the annual ski trip. Even though the flu almost wiped me out I made a speedy recovery. Mom finded *found* a great deal on a plane ticket for me and I flied *flew* to Orlando with her. I got a surprise summer vacation this winter!

warm regards
Morgan

Error Summary

Capitalization	3
Language Usage	2
Punctuation:	
Comma	4

THURSDAY   **WEEK 25**

Name _____

orlando Florida

January 5 2004

dear Nick

   I know you're not going to believe me but I promise you that I'm tell you the truth! i'm here in florida spending a few days with my cousins. My mom and I flew here on january 2nd and I'll be home the day before school starts

WATCH FOR

- letter (greeting)
- commas

WEDNESDAY   **WEEK 25**

   Mom had to go to a conference in orlando for her job. of course I was supposed to be gone on the annual ski trip. Even though the flu almost wiped me out I made a speedy recovery. Mom finded a great deal on a plane ticket for me and I flied to Orlando with her. I got a surprise summer vacation this winter!

   warm regards

   Morgan

WATCH FOR

- verb tenses

THURSDAY   **WEEK 25**

Preview the 4 daily lessons to ensure you review or introduce skills that may be unfamiliar to students.

The Science Project

just before the bell rang mr. Nielsen said, "Don't forget that your science projects are ~~do~~ due a week from today."

Mario thought about his project. A few days before he found frog eggs at the pond near his house. He used a jar to scoop up some pond water along with the clear jelly-like frog eggs. at home, he put the jar on top of the refrigerator to stay warm The eggs looked like slippery shiny dark ~~beads~~ beads in clear jelly.

Error Summary	
Capitalization	3
Punctuation:	
Comma	5
Period	1
Quotation Mark	1
Other	1
Spelling	2

MONDAY   **WEEK 26**

---

each day, mario looked at the eggs through a magnifying glass drew what he saw and made notes in a journal. day by day, he ~~watch~~ watched the jelly part of the eggs get smaller as the tadpoles grew in the black centers. He could soon see heads and ~~tales~~ tails and the tadpoles began to move his science book said that the jelly part was food for the growing tadpoles. "I sure hope they have all the food they need, Mario thought to ~~hisself~~ himself.

Error Summary	
Capitalization	4
Language Usage	2
Punctuation:	
Comma	3
Period	2
Quotation Mark	1
Spelling	1

TUESDAY   **WEEK 26**

The Science Project

just before the bell rang mr. Nielsen said, "Don't forget that your science projects are do a week from today.

Mario thought about his project. A few days before he found frog eggs at the pond near his house. He used a jar to scoop up some pond water along with the clear jelly like frog eggs. at home, he put the jar on top of the refrigerator to stay warm The eggs looked like slippery shiny dark beeds in clear jelly.

- hyphens
- commas

each day, mario looked at the eggs through a magnifying glass drew what he saw and made notes in a journal. day by day, he watch the jelly part of the eggs get smaller as the tadpoles grew in the black centers. He could soon see heads and tales and the tadpoles began to move his science book said that the jelly part was food for the growing tadpoles. "I sure hope they have all the food they need, Mario thought to hisself

- pronouns
- quotes

The next ~~thursday~~ thursday, the first egg ~~hached~~ hatched. A tiny tadpole moved about in the water. "I think it's time to add some plant life to this water," Mario said as he headed off to the pond.

As soon as he placed the pond plants in the water, the tiny tadpole ~~sticked~~ stuck itself to a leaf. Even though he looked through his magnifying glass, mario couldn't see ~~it's~~ its mouth. he could just barely see its tiny fine see-through gills.

WEDNESDAY   **WEEK 26**

Error Summary	
Capitalization	3
Language Usage	1
Punctuation:	
Apostrophe	2
Comma	4
Period	3
Quotation Mark	1
Other	1
Spelling	1

mario organized his day-by-day drawings, journal notes, and the other materials to take to school. By early friday morning, four more eggs had hatched. mario packed everything into a cardboard box and carried it carefully to school.

As mario ~~begun~~ began to unpack his project box, mr. nielsen glanced over his shoulder. "it looks like you were able to do some real scientific observations. I can't wait to hear all about it!" he said.

THURSDAY   **WEEK 26**

Error Summary	
Capitalization	7
Language Usage	1
Punctuation:	
Comma	4
Period	2
Quotation Mark	2

The next thursday, the first egg hached. A tiny tadpole moved about in the water "I think its time to add some plant life to this water, Mario said as he headed off to the pond.

As soon as he placed the pond plants in the water the tiny tadpole sticked itself to a leaf. Even though he looked through his magnifying glass mario couldn't see it's mouth he could just barely see its tiny fine see through gills

- apostrophes
- hyphens

WEDNESDAY   **WEEK 26**

mario organized his day-by-day drawings journal notes and the other materials to take to school. By early friday morning four more eggs had hatched. mario packed everything into a cardboard box and carried it carefully to school.

As mario begun to unpack his project box mr nielsen glanced over his shoulder. it looks like you were able to do some real scientific observations I can't wait to hear all about it! he said.

- abbreviations
- quotes

THURSDAY   **WEEK 26**

Preview the 4 daily lessons to ensure you review or introduce skills that may be unfamiliar to students.

Seashore Mystery

my family and I spend summer vacations in Havenport. We stay at Uncle clay and aunt anita's beach house. Ricky my younger brother and I play in the tide pools we look for the creatures that hide between and under the rocks. Our parents watch us from the deck and call out things like, "Carefull! Here comes a big wave! and did you put sunscreen on your ears?" that's how our days usually go but one day something really unusual happening

Careful

happened

Error Summary	
Capitalization	7
Language Usage	1
Punctuation:	
Comma	5
Period	2
Quotation Mark	2
Other	1
Spelling	1

MONDAY　　　　　　　　　　　　**WEEK 27**

The best time to look for sea creatures is in the morning ricky carries the bucket and I lifts the rocks. We never keep any of the animals we catch we only look at them for a while and then put them back there is one creature that I will never forget. ricky saw it first and said "Ted come hear quickly! I ran over to where he was standing I could see long silver claws gripping the side of a rock

lift

here

Error Summary	
Capitalization	4
Language Usage	1
Punctuation:	
Comma	3
Period	5
Quotation Mark	1
Spelling	1

TUESDAY　　　　　　　　　　　　**WEEK 27**

Name _____

Seashore Mystery

my family and I spend summer vacations in Havenport. We stay at Uncle clay and aunt anita's beach house. Ricky my younger brother and I play in the tide pools we look for the creatures that hide between and under the rocks. Our parents watch us from the deck and call out things like "Carefull! Here comes a big wave! and did you put sunscreen on your ears" that's how our days usually go but one day something really unusual happening

MONDAY   **WEEK 27**

The best time to look for sea creatures is in the morning ricky carries the bucket and I lifts the rocks. We never keep any of the animals we catch we only look at them for a while and then put them back there is one creature that I will never forget. ricky saw it first and said "Ted come hear quickly! I ran over to where he was standing I could see long silver claws gripping the side of a rock

TUESDAY   **WEEK 27**

a shiver ran through my body as I leaned over to see more Its scales were a brilliant, sparkling yellow and its skin was the color of green slime it was be like nothing I had ever seen before. "ricky go get Mom and Dad and youd better hurry!" I leaned closer to the rock to get a better look. Suddenly, the thing's head moved and I saw three purple eyes looking straight strate into mine "Where is it Ted? Is it still there?" Ricky called.

Error Summary

Capitalization	3
Language Usage	1
Punctuation:	
Apostrophe	1
Comma	6
Period	4
Quotation Mark	2
Other	1
Spelling	1

WEDNESDAY　　　　　　　　　　　　WEEK 27

mom and dad were was close behind Ricky. "Dad, look at this" The creatures silver claws still held tightly onto the rock, and its three eyes stared at us. "I think it's stuck" said Dad. "Let's lift the rock" The creature gave a yelp as we began to lift the heavy, wet rock. As soon as we did, the strange creature immediately disappeared disapeared into the incoming tide. Its lean, slippery, whipping tail was the last thing we saw as it slipped away.

Error Summary

Capitalization	2
Language Usage	1
Punctuation:	
Apostrophe	2
Comma	7
Period	3
Quotation Mark	2
Spelling	1

THURSDAY　　　　　　　　　　　　WEEK 27

a shiver ran through my body as I leaned over to see more Its scales were a brilliant sparkling yellow and its skin was the color of green slime it be like nothing I had ever seen before. ricky go get Mom and Dad and youd better hurry!" I leaned closer to the rock to get a better look. Suddenly, the thing's head moved and I saw three purple eyes looking strate into mine "Where is it Ted? Is it still there Ricky called

• quotes

WEDNESDAY   **WEEK 27**

mom and dad was close behind Ricky. "Dad look at this" The creatures silver claws still held tightly onto the rock and its three eyes stared at us. I think it's stuck" said Dad. "Lets lift the rock The creature gave a yelp as we began to lift the heavy wet rock. As soon as we did the strange creature immediately disapeared into the incoming tide. Its lean slippery whipping tail was the last thing we saw as it slipped away

• commas
• quotes

THURSDAY   **WEEK 27**

Preview the 4 daily lessons to ensure you review or introduce skills that may be unfamiliar to students.

Dinotopia

where can you ~~reed~~ read about humans and intelligent dinosaurs that have lived together for centuries? You can in james Gurney's series of books about a land of intelligent dinosaurs the first book in the series, <u>Dinotopia: A Land Apart from Time</u> introduces readers to biologist and explorer Arthur denison and his son will who are shipwrecked on a hidden island. there they encounter intelligent dinosaurs living in ~~harmonee~~ harmony with marooned travelers

Error Summary

Capitalization	6
Punctuation:	
Comma	1
Period	2
Spelling	2

MONDAY   **WEEK 28**

The denison's are taken to an amazing world where ~~citys~~ cities are ~~bilt~~ built on waterfalls and people have found a way to fly The dinosaurs on this island are unusual, to say the least. in fact they speak seven languages use tools and have their own form of writing. they are peaceful intelligent herbivores, each with a unique personality. the humans on the island communicate with the dinosaurs and work ~~togeter~~ together with them to build an ideal city

Error Summary

Capitalization	4
Punctuation:	
Comma	4
Period	2
Spelling	4

TUESDAY   **WEEK 28**

Dinotopia

where can you reed about humans and intelligent dinosaurs that have lived together for centuries? You can in james Gurney's series of books about a land of intelligent dinosaurs the first book in the series, <u>Dinotopia: A Land Apart from Time</u> introduces readers to biologist and explorer Arthur denison and his son will who are shipwrecked on a hidden island. there they encounter intelligent dinosaurs living in harmonee with marooned travelers

• spelling

MONDAY   **WEEK 28**

The denison's are taken to an amazing world where citys are bilt on waterfalls and people have found a way to fly The dinosaurs on this island are unusual, to say the least. in fact they speak seven languages use tools and have their own form of writing. they are peaceful intelligent herbivores, each with a unique personality. the humans on the island communicate with the dinosaurs and work togeter with them to build an ideal city

• spelling
• commas

TUESDAY   **WEEK 28**

will and his dad experience many exciting adventures on the island of dinotopia. you must read James gurneys next book, dinotopia: The world beneath, to find out how Will and his dad travel to an ancient place at the very heart of Dinotopia. Another book written by james Gurney is Dinotopia: First Flight. In this book Mr. Gurney introduces readers to a whole new world from Dinotopias ancient past.

Error Summary

Capitalization	8
Punctuation:	
Apostrophe	2
Comma	1
Other	1

WEDNESDAY **WEEK 28**

There are a lot of books about Dinotopia, many of which are written by various authors For example Dinotopia: river quest is written by John vornholt. Another title, Hatchling, is written by Midori snyder. With so many ~~book~~ books in the series, you can read about dinotopia all year long but you'd better be careful not to get permanently lost in the adventure and excitement in the land of dinotopia

Error Summary

Capitalization	6
Language Usage	1
Punctuation:	
Comma	2
Period	2
Other	1

THURSDAY **WEEK 28**

EMC 2728 • Daily Paragraph Editing, Grade 5 • ©2004 by Evan-Moor Corp.

will and his dad experience many exciting adventures on the island of dinotopia. you must read James gurneys next book, <u>dinotopia: The world beneath,</u> to find out how Will and his dad travel to an ancient place at the very heart of Dinotopia. Another book written by james Gurney is Dinotopia: First Flight. In this book Mr. Gurney introduces readers to a whole new world from Dinotopias ancient past.

• book titles

WEDNESDAY   **WEEK 28**

There are a lot of books about Dinotopia, many of which are written by various authors For example <u>Dinotopia: river quest</u> is written by John vornholt. Another title, Hatchling, is written by Midori snyder. With so many book in the series, you can read about dinotopia all year long but you'd better be careful not to get permanently lost in the adventure and excitement in the land of dinotopia

• names of places
• book titles

THURSDAY   **WEEK 28**

Preview the 4 daily lessons to ensure you review or introduce skills that may be unfamiliar to students.

Waverly Residents Prepare for Tornadoes

Error Summary	
Capitalization	8
Language Usage	1
Punctuation:	
Apostrophe	2
Comma	5
Period	2
Spelling	1

wednesday august 7 1997

Waverly residents crowded into city hall last night, anxious to hear a presentation given by the Red Cross. red cross officials distributed waverlys community disaster plan and answered questions from concerned residents last years tornadoes rocked this community and although they left as quickly as they came waverly is still reeling from the damage. as tornado season approaches city officials are stressing tornado preparedness

MONDAY   **WEEK 29**

Error Summary	
Capitalization	4
Punctuation:	
Comma	9
Period	4
Other	1
Spelling	1

over 500 people stood in line for hours, determined to get red Cross tornado kits The kits include first-aid supplies flashlights matches candles water bottles canned food blankets batteries and radios In addition to the kits over 300 walkie-talkies donated by Communications R Us were distributed to residents many people attended Waverly medical Center's various CPR demonstrations, which took place throughout the evening

TUESDAY   **WEEK 29**

Name _____

Waverly Residents Prepare for Tornadoes

wednesday august 7 1997

Waverly residents crowded into city hall last night, anxious to heer a presentation given by the Red Cross. red cross officials distributed waverlys community disaster plan and answered questions from concerned residents last years tornadoes rocked this community and although they left as quickly as they came waverly is still reeling from the damage. as tornado season approaches city officials is stressing tornado preparedness

- commas
- apostrophes

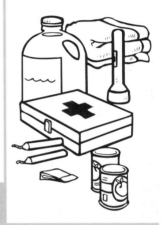

MONDAY	WEEK 29

over 500 people stood in line for hours, determined to get red Cross tornado kits The kits include first aid supplies flashlights matches candles water bottles canned food blankets batteries and radios In addition to the kits over 300 walkie-talkies donatted by Communications R Us were distributed to residents many people attended Waverly medical Center's various CPR demonstrations, which took place throughout the evening

- commas
- hyphens

TUESDAY	WEEK 29

at last night's meeting mayor finley announced that the waverly City Council unanimously approved ~~aproved~~ the plan for a tornado warning system the system consists of a warning siren and emergency lights volunteers with electrical and construction knowledge are needed ~~neded~~ to help install the system several sirens will be placed in strategic locations throughout waverly A practice drill will be scheduled once the system is put into place

WEDNESDAY **WEEK 29**

Error Summary

Capitalization	8
Punctuation:	
Apostrophe	1
Comma	1
Period	5
Spelling	2

several disaster preparedness drives are ~~is~~ taking place during the month of august Members of waverly's rescue team will be out in full force on saturday august 10 their goal is to recruit and train at least 20 new members The waverly County Food Bank is conducting a nonperishable food drive cereal dried fruit and powdered milk are needed the community is encouraged to continue to support disaster preparedness efforts ~~eforts~~

THURSDAY **WEEK 29**

Error Summary

Capitalization	9
Language Usage	1
Punctuation:	
Apostrophe	1
Comma	3
Period	6
Spelling	1

Name _____

at last nights meeting mayor finley announced that the waverly City Council unanimously aproved the plan for a tornado warning system the system consists of a warning siren and emergency lights volunteers with electrical and construction knowledge are neded to help install the system several sirens will be placed in strategic locations throughout waverly A practice drill will be scheduled once the system is put into place

• run-on sentences

WEDNESDAY   **WEEK 29**

several disaster preparedness drives is taking place during the month of august Members of waverlys rescue team will be out in full force on saturday august 10 their goal is to recruit and train at least 20 new members The waverly County Food Bank is conducting a nonperishable food drive cereal dried fruit and powdered milk are needed the community is encouraged to continue to support disaster preparedness eforts

• run-on sentences

THURSDAY   **WEEK 29**

Preview the 4 daily lessons to ensure you review or introduce skills that may be unfamiliar to students.

Your Fair Share

Grenada Cleanup <u>Recycle for Life</u> magazine's top-notch reporter has done it again! ms Cleanup has crossed the <u>united</u> <u>states</u> asking kids about their conservation habits. she wanted to find out if today's kids are taking more than their fair share from the planet. Heres an excerpt from her interview with mr tapan's fifth-grade class, an outstanding group of young recyclers

Error Summary	
Capitalization	6
Punctuation:	
Apostrophe	1
Comma	2
Period	3
Other	1

MONDAY **WEEK 30**

Ms. Cleanup (GC): wesley can you tell the <u>Recycle for Life</u> readers what you do to conserve our planets resources?

Wesley: I'd be happy to ms. Cleanup. Shall I call you ms cleanup, or do you prefer grenada?

GC: Ms Cleanup will be fine wesley

Wesley: Well Ms. Cleanup I conserve water. I turn the water off while I brush my teeth and while I shampoo my hair

Error Summary	
Capitalization	5
Punctuation:	
Apostrophe	1
Comma	5
Period	4
Other	2

TUESDAY **WEEK 30**

EMC 2728 • Daily Paragraph Editing, Grade 5 • ©2004 by Evan-Moor Corp.

Your Fair Share

Grenada Cleanup <u>Recycle for Life</u> magazine's top-notch reporter has done it again! ms Cleanup has crossed the united states asking kids about their conservation habits. she wanted to find out if today's kids are taking more than their fair share from the planet. Heres an excerpt from her interview with mr tapan's fifth grade class, an outstanding group of young recyclers

- abbreviations
- hyphens

MONDAY **WEEK 30**

Ms. Cleanup (GC): wesley can you tell the Recycle for Life readers what you do to conserve our planets resources

Wesley: I'd be happy to ms. Cleanup. Shall I call you ms cleanup, or do you prefer grenada?

GC: Ms Cleanup will be fine wesley

Wesley: Well Ms. Cleanup I conserve water. I turn the water off while I brush my teeth and while I shampoo my hair

- magazine titles
- abbreviations

TUESDAY **WEEK 30**

GC: Fantastic! water conservation is very important,
Wesley. domenic how do you conserve our planets
resources?

Domenic: Since I live about a mile from school I've
decided to ride my bike to school and conserve
nonrenewable resources like gasoline

GC: Now youre talking! Recycle for Life knows
that reducing pollution and conserving resources
are major challenges for our nation.

WEDNESDAY   **WEEK 30**

GC: Tam, what are your conservation strategies?

Tam: I recycle plastic paper and aluminum. My family
buys napkins paper towels and other products made
from recycled materials. I like to help conserve
Earths resources.

GC: Recycle for Life applauds Mr tapan's class.
they are terrific role models for adults and
kids who want to do their fair share for
the environment

THURSDAY   **WEEK 30**

GC: Fantastic! water conservation is very important Wesley. domenic how do you conserve our planets resources

Domenic: Since I live about a mile from school I've decided to ride my bike to school and conserve nonrenewable resources like gasoline

GC: Now youre talking! Recycle for Life knows that reducing pollution and conserving resources are major challenges for our nation.

- apostrophes
- magazine titles

WEDNESDAY   **WEEK 30**

GC: Tam, what are your conservation strategies

Tam: I recycle plastic paper and aluminum. My family buys napkins paper towels and other products made from recycled materials. I like to help conserve Earths resources.

GC: Recycle for Life applauds Mr tapan's class. they are terrific role models for adults and kids who want to do their fair share for the environment

- commas
- magazine titles

THURSDAY   **WEEK 30**

Preview the 4 daily lessons to ensure you review or introduce skills that may be unfamiliar to students.

How to Make Saltwater Taffy

Saltwater taffy is easy to make. What isn't so easy, on the other hand, is trying not to eat it before it's finished! you will need these ingredients: 3 cups sugar, 1 cup water, 1 cup light corn syrup, 4 tablespoons butter, 1½ teaspoons vanilla extract, and 1 teaspoon salt. it is helpful to use a candy ~~canndy~~ thermometer. however, you can also check to see if the taffy is ready by dropping a small amount of it into cold water. if it forms a hard ball, it is ready.

Error Summary	
Capitalization	4
Punctuation:	
Apostrophe	2
Comma	9
Period	2
Spelling	1

MONDAY　　　　　　　　**WEEK 31**

---

before you begin mixing the ingredients, butter a square pan. combine the sugar, corn syrup, salt, and water in a 2quart saucepan. cook on low heat, stirring constantly until the sugar dissolves. Next, allow the mixture to cook for about 30 minutes or until the candy thermometer reaches 256°. remember, you can try ~~tri~~ dropping a small amount into cold water ~~watter~~ to see if it forms a hard ball. remove the saucepan from the stove. Be careful; it will be hot.

Error Summary	
Capitalization	5
Punctuation:	
Comma	4
Period	3
Other	1
Spelling	2

TUESDAY　　　　　　　　**WEEK 31**

How to Make Saltwater Taffy

Saltwater taffy is easy to make What isnt so easy on the other hand is trying not to eat it before its finished! you will need these ingredients: 3 cups sugar 1 cup water 1 cup light corn syrup 4 tablespoons butter 1½ teaspoons vanilla extract and 1 teaspoon salt. it is helpful to use a canndy thermometer. however you can also check to see if the taffy is ready by dropping a small amount of it into cold water if it forms a hard ball it is ready.

MONDAY   **WEEK 31**

before you begin mixing the ingredients butter a square pan. combine the sugar corn syrup salt and water in a 2quart saucepan. cook on low heat, stirring constantly until the sugar dissolves Next, allow the mixture to cook for about 30 minutes or until the candy thermometer reaches 256°. remember, you can tri dropping a small amount into cold watter to see if it forms a hard ball remove the saucepan from the stove. Be careful; it will be hot

TUESDAY   **WEEK 31**

now, add the butter and vanilla to the mixture you may want to add food coloring to this recipe if so, now ~~are~~ *is* the perfect time Stir all the ingredients together until they ~~is~~ *are* evenly distributed. pour the mixture into the buttered pan lightly coat your ~~hans~~ *hands* with butter this step is called "butter fingers" When the mixture or taffy, is just cool enough to handle pull it into long strips one-half-inch wide. cut pieces one and one-half-inches long

Error Summary

Capitalization	7
Language Usage	2
Punctuation:	
Comma	2
Period	7
Quotation Mark	1
Other	2
Spelling	1

WEDNESDAY　　　　　　**WEEK 31**

---

finally, tightly wrap the individual taffy pieces in waxed paper. this last step is very important in fact the taffy will not hold its shape unless it is wrapped tightly

Why call it "saltwater taffy" when it only contains 1 teaspoon of salt? By most accounts, the name was coined after a vendor on atlantic city's boardwalk had his supply of taffy damaged by a storm tide. He decided to sell the taffy under the name "saltwater taffy," it seems the name "stuck"

Error Summary

Capitalization	6
Punctuation:	
Comma	1
Period	4
Quotation Mark	3
Other	1

THURSDAY　　　　　　**WEEK 31**

Name _____

now, add the butter and vanilla to the mixture you may want to add food coloring to this recipe if so, now are the perfect time Stir all the ingredients together until they is evenly distributed. pour the mixture into the buttered pan lightly coat your hans with butter this step is called butter fingers" When the mixture or taffy, is just cool enough to handle pull it into long strips one-half inch wide. cut pieces one and one-half inches long

- hyphens
- verb tenses

WEDNESDAY   **WEEK 31**

---

finally, tightly wrap the individual taffy pieces in waxed paper. this last step is very important in fact the taffy will not hold its shape unless it is wrapped tightly

Why call it saltwater taffy" when it only contains 1 teaspoon of salt By most accounts, the name was coined after a vendor on atlantic city's boardwalk had his supply of taffy damaged by a storm tide. He decided to sell the taffy under the name "saltwater taffy, it seems the name "stuck

- special words in quotes
- question marks

THURSDAY   **WEEK 31**

Preview the 4 daily lessons to ensure you review or introduce skills that may be unfamiliar to students.

The Pull of the Pole

Ernest Shackleton was born in ireland in 1874. his family moved to england when he was a child, and Shackleton continued his studies there. at the age of 16, shackleton left school to follow his ~~dreem~~ dream of adventure at sea he signed on to a commercial ship that was headed for south america. The ship reached Cape Horn in the middle of the winter the crew spent more than two months navigating around the Horn

Error Summary	
Capitalization	9
Punctuation:	
Period	3
Spelling	1

MONDAY   **WEEK 32**

this dramatic trip awakened in Shackleton a longing to travel to the South Pole nevertheless, he continued to work for ~~yeers~~ years as a sailor and he also trained to become a ships commander. In 1913 at age 39, shackleton realized his dream. he bought his own boat which he named _Endurance_ and began to plan his expedition to the south pole. He hired a big crew he took 27 men, 69 sled dogs, and one cat named Mr. Chippy

Error Summary	
Capitalization	7
Punctuation:	
Apostrophe	1
Comma	3
Period	3
Spelling	1

TUESDAY   **WEEK 32**

EMC 2728 • Daily Paragraph Editing, Grade 5 • ©2004 by Evan-Moor Corp.

The Pull of the Pole

Ernest Shackleton was born in ireland in 1874. his family moved to england when he was a child, and Shackleton continued his studies there. at the age of 16, shackleton left school to follow his dreem of adventure at sea he signed on to a commercial ship that was headed for south america. The ship reached Cape Horn in the middle of the winter the crew spent more than two months navigating around the Horn

• names of places

MONDAY   **WEEK 32**

this dramatic trip awakened in Shackleton a longing to travel to the South Pole nevertheless, he continued to work for yeers as a sailor and he also trained to become a ships commander. In 1913 at age 39, shackleton realized his dream. he bought his own boat which he named <u>Endurance</u> and began to plan his expedition to the south pole. He hired a big crew he took 27 men, 69 sled dogs, and one cat named Mr. Chippy

• run-on sentences

TUESDAY   **WEEK 32**

the ship set ~~sale~~ *sail* from england on august 8 1914. After 14 months at sea the <u>Endurance</u> got stuck in ice. The crew tried to chip the ice away but it didn't work Soon the boat sprang leaks Shackleton ordered everyone to abandon ship. In november, the <u>Endurance</u> broke up due to the pressure of the ice. it sank to the bottom of the sea. for the next 4½ months shackleton and his crew lived on the ice. They had to find land or they would die

Error Summary	
Capitalization	7
Punctuation:	
Apostrophe	1
Comma	4
Period	3
Other	1
Spelling	1

WEDNESDAY   **WEEK 32**

shackleton and his crew ventured out to sea in three lifeboats they salvaged from the <u>Endurance</u> after six treacherous days they landed on a cold windy uninhabited island. Conditions were harsh Shackleton came up with a plan to reach a tiny island where he ~~now~~ *knew* there was a whaling station it took him and five of his crew 17 days to reach the island amazingly, all 27 crew members were rescued and they all arrived home unharmed

Error Summary	
Capitalization	4
Punctuation:	
Comma	4
Period	5
Other	1
Spelling	1

THURSDAY   **WEEK 32**

the ship set sale from england on august 8 1914. After 14 months at sea the <u>Endurance</u> got stuck in ice. The crew tried to chip the ice away but it didnt work Soon the boat sprang leaks Shackleton ordered everyone to abandon ship. In november, the Endurance broke up due to the pressure of the ice. it sank to the bottom of the sea. for the next 4½ months shackleton and his crew lived on the ice. They had to find land or they would die

WATCH FOR

• names of ships
• names of months

WEDNESDAY   **WEEK 32**

shackleton and his crew ventured out to sea in three lifeboats they salvaged from the Endurance after six treacherous days they landed on a cold windy uninhabited island. Conditions were harsh Shackleton came up with a plan to reach a tiny island where he new there was a whaling station it took him and five of his crew 17 days to reach the island amazingly, all 27 crew members were rescued and they all arrived home unharmed

WATCH FOR

• names of ships
• run-on sentences

THURSDAY   **WEEK 32**

Preview the 4 daily lessons to ensure you review or introduce skills that may be unfamiliar to students.

Roving the Red Planet

You may have heard of a dog named rover but
have you ever ~~herd~~ heard of a rover named Spirit? That is
what scientists at NASA have named a golf-cart-size
robotic explorer that ~~were~~ was launched in june 2003 on
a seven-month voyage to mars. Opportunity, a second
rover was also sent into space early in july 2003 both
rovers are scheduled to land on the Red Planet in
january 2004.

Error Summary

Capitalization	6
Language Usage	1
Punctuation:	
Comma	2
Period	2
Other	3
Spelling	1

MONDAY   **WEEK 33**

Once the two rovers arrive on mars they will
act as robotic geologists. Each rover is equipped with
a drill that can cut into rock to ~~removed~~ remove samples.
Panoramic cameras are mounted on the rovers, giving
NASA scientists on Earth closeup views of rocks on
the planet's surface 399 kilometers (248 mi.) away.
The rovers will move over the martian surface on six
wheels? The data they collect will be transmitted back
to ~~sientists~~ scientists on earth.

Error Summary

Capitalization	3
Language Usage	1
Punctuation:	
Comma	1
Period	1
Spelling	1

TUESDAY   **WEEK 33**

Name _____

Roving the Red Planet

You may have heard of a dog named rover but have you ever herd of a rover named <u>Spirit</u>. That is what scientists at NASA have named a golf-cart-size robotic explorer that were launched in june 2003 on a seven=month voyage to mars. Opportunity, a second rover was also sent into space early in july 2003 both rovers are scheduled to land on the Red Planet in january 2004

WATCH FOR

• names of spacecraft
• hyphens

MONDAY   **WEEK 33**

Once the two rovers arrive on mars they will act as robotic geologists. Each rover is equipped with a drill that can cut into rock to removed samples. Panoramic cameras are mounted on the rovers, giving NASA scientists on Earth closeup views of rocks on the planet's surface 399 kilometers (248 mi.) away. The rovers will move over the martian surface on six wheels? The data they collect will be transmitted back to sientists on earth.

WATCH FOR

• names of planets

TUESDAY   **WEEK 33**

Opportunity and spirit are scheduled to land on opposite sides of mars. The two landing sites were chosen because they might provide clues about past water activity on mars. Previous missions to mars has gathered evidence showing the presents of water on mars in the past? Scientists are now hoping to learn how much water there was on the Red planet and find out when it disapeared.

Editing marks shown: chosen (replacing choosed), have (replacing has), presence (replacing presents), disappeared (replacing disapeared); capitalization marks under mars; period/question mark corrections

Error Summary

Capitalization	6
Language Usage	2
Punctuation:	
Period	1
Other	1
Spelling	2

WEDNESDAY   **WEEK 33**

For years, scientists and the public in general has been intrigued by the possibility of life on mars. In fact, recent examination of a martian meteorite found in antarctica in 1982 showed evidence of primitive cellular life-forms on the red Planet. Scientists will use the latest high powered electron microscopes to examine the rock samples gathered by the rovers perhaps new discoverys about life on mars will be possible

Editing marks shown: have (replacing has), discoveries (replacing discoverys); capitalization marks; period and other punctuation corrections

Error Summary

Capitalization	6
Language Usage	1
Punctuation:	
Period	2
Other	1
Spelling	1

THURSDAY   **WEEK 33**

Name _____

Opportunity and <u>spirit</u> are scheduled to land on opposite sides of mars. The two landing sites were choosed because they might provide clues about past water activity on mars. Previous missions to mars has gathered evidence showing the presents of water on mars in the past? Scientists are now hoping to learn how much water there was on the Red planet and find out when it disapeared.

WATCH FOR

- names of spacecraft
- spelling

WEDNESDAY   **WEEK 33**

For years, scientists and the public in general has been intrigued by the possibility of life on mars. In fact, recent examination of a martian meteorite found in antarctica in 1982 showed evidence of primitive cellular life-forms on the red Planet. Scientists will use the latest high/powered electron microscopes to examine the rock samples gathered by the rovers perhaps new discoverys about life on mars will be possible

WATCH FOR

- hyphens

THURSDAY   **WEEK 33**

Preview the 4 daily lessons to ensure you review or introduce skills that may be unfamiliar to students.

A Fascinating Character

We get to know Mila, the narrator and main character in karen hesse's novel The music of the dolphins through her journal entries. They make up most of this fascinating unusual novel.

Two other short sections at the beginning of the book help set the stage for the story in the first three pages mila describes a peaceful day of swimming with her "dolphin cousins" until she is unexpectedly captured by a man who arrives by plane.

Error Summary

Capitalization	6
Punctuation:	
Comma	3
Period	3
Quotation Mark	1
Spelling	1

MONDAY   **WEEK 34**

---

the other section that precedes the journal entries is a realistic two-page "newspaper article." It describes how a "wild child" has been picked up by the Coast Guard on an isolated remote island between florida and cuba. For the rest of the book we read journal entries written by this "wild child, Mila.

Milas first journal entries are written in odd simple language its clear that shes just beginning to learn english.

Error Summary

Capitalization	5
Punctuation:	
Apostrophe	3
Comma	4
Period	1
Quotation Mark	1
Spelling	1

TUESDAY   **WEEK 34**

EMC 2728 • Daily Paragraph Editing, Grade 5 • ©2004 by Evan-Moor Corp.

A Fascinating Character

We get to know Mila, the narrator and main caracter in karen hesse's novel <u>The music of the dolphins</u> through her journal entries. They make up most of this fascinating unusual novel

Two other short sections at the beginning of the book help set the stage for the story in the first three pages mila describes a peaceful day of swimming with her "dolphin cousins until she is unexpectedly captured by a man who arrives by plane

WATCH FOR

- special words in quotes

MONDAY   **WEEK 34**

the other section that precedes the journal entries is a realistic two-page "newspaper article." It describes how a "wild child" has been picked up by the Coast Guard on an isolated remote island between florida and cuba. For the rest of the book we read jornal entries written by this "wild child, Mila.

Milas first journal entries are written in odd simple language its clear that shes just beginning to learn english.

WATCH FOR

- apostrophes

TUESDAY   **WEEK 34**

as the journal entries progress we learn that from an early age mila has lived on her island and has been cared for by her dolphin "family. The dolphins saved mila when her family was lost at sea

After the Coast guard "rescue" Mila is cared for by kind gentle doctors who are anxious to study her adjustment to life with humans and to see how she learns to communicate in English we are able to watch these changes through her journal entries.

Error Summary

Capitalization	5
Language Usage	1
Punctuation:	
Comma	3
Period	2
Quotation Mark	1

WEDNESDAY   **WEEK 34**

As Milas journal entries get longer we see her as a caring thoughtful girl who is anxious to connect with Sandy, one of the researchers and Dr. Beck, who heads the ~~reserch~~ research team. mila also has a special friendship with justin Dr. Beck's teenage son who is struggling to find his own identity and break away from his overprotective mother Milas challenge is to figure out how she fits into the world and her struggle to do so makes this a moving story

Error Summary

Capitalization	2
Punctuation:	
Apostrophe	2
Comma	6
Period	2
Spelling	1

THURSDAY   **WEEK 34**

Name _____

as the journal entries progress we learn that from an early age mila has lived on her island and been cared for by her dolphin "family. The dolphins saved mila when her family was lost at sea

After the Coast guard "rescue" Mila is cared for by kind gentle doctors who are anxious to study her adjustment to life with humans and to see how she learns to communicate in English we are able to watch these changes through her journal entries.

- special words in quotes

WEDNESDAY   **WEEK 34**

As Milas journal entries get longer we see her as a caring thoughtful girl who is anxious to connect with Sandy, one of the researchers and Dr. Beck, who heads the reserch team. mila also has a special friendship with justin Dr. Beck's teenage son who is struggling to find his own identity and break away from his overprotective mother Milas challenge is to figure out how she fits into the world and her struggle to do so makes this a moving story

- apostrophes
- commas

THURSDAY   **WEEK 34**

Preview the 4 daily lessons to ensure you review or introduce skills that may be unfamiliar to students.

Raceway Rockets

It may seem ~~od~~ odd to compare race-car drivers to astronauts, but as you learn about how the force of gravity affects people in these two high/speed professions, the similarities become more obvious. This force, known as "G-force" is a feeling of increased weight that occurs during acceleration. You have probably ~~feeled~~ felt it when you've careened downhill on a roller coaster, and your stomach seemed to drop to your knees?

Error Summary

Language Usage	1
Punctuation:	
Comma	3
Period	1
Other	1
Spelling	1

MONDAY **WEEK 35**

The force of three G's feels something like two men sitting on your chest during blastoff, astronauts may experience from three to seven G's of acceleration. Race/car drivers, on the other hand, experience more than four G's, often for as long as two solid hours. G-force can push on any side of the driver's body driver's feel G-force on the front of their bodies when they accelerate, on the back when they brake, and on either side when they turn.

Error Summary

Capitalization	2
Punctuation:	
Apostrophe	1
Comma	4
Period	2
Other	2
Spelling	1

TUESDAY **WEEK 35**

Raceway Rockets

It may seem od to compare race-car drivers to astronauts but as you learn about how the force of gravity affects people in these two high/speed professions, the similarities become more obvious. This force, known as "G-force" is a feeling of increased weight that occurs during acceleration. You have probably felt it when you've careened downhill on a roller coaster and your stomach seemed to drop to your knees?

• commas

MONDAY   **WEEK 35**

The force of three G's feels something like two men sitting on your chest during blastoff, astronauts may experience from three to seven G's of acceleration. Race.car drivers on the other hand experience more than four G's, often for as long as two solid hours. G-force can push on any side of the drivers body driver's feel G force on the front of their bodies when they accelerate on the back when they brake and on either side when they turn.

• hyphens

TUESDAY   **WEEK 35**

During takeoff, an astronauts heart usually beats around 100 times per minute. A race-car driver's heart can beat up to 200 times per minute, similar to the 175 beats per minute averaged by marathon runner's during a race. By contrast, the resting heartbeat for typical adult's is 60 to 80 beets per minute. This is one reason why phisycal conditioning has become almost as important for race car drivers as it is for astronauts.

Error Summary

Punctuation:
Apostrophe	1
Other	2
Spelling	5

WEDNESDAY   WEEK 35

Like astronauts, race car drivers now use a sophisticated assortment of protective gear for both, protective helmets also contain two way communication systems. Astronauts stay in touch with Mission Control, while drivers can talk to race engineers Astronauts suits are fireproof, waterproof, airtight, ventilated, and protect against extreme temperatures drivers' suits can withstand up to 1,300 degrees Fahrenheit! Ready, set go...blast off?!

Error Summary

Capitalization	2
Punctuation:	
Apostrophe	1
Comma	5
Period	3
Other	3

THURSDAY   WEEK 35

Name _____

During takeoff, an astronauts heart usually beats around 100 times per minute. A race=car driver's heart can beat up to 200 times per minute, similar to the 175 beats per minute averaged by marathon runner's during a race. By contrast, the resting heartbeat for typical adult's is 60 to 80 beets per minute. This is one reason why phisycal conditioning has become almost as important for race/car drivers as it is for astronauts'.

WEDNESDAY   **WEEK 35**

Like astronauts, race.car drivers now use a sophisticated assortment of protective gear for both, protective helmets also contain two/way communication systems. Astronauts stay in touch with Mission Control, while drivers can talk to race engineers Astronauts suits are fireproof waterproof airtight ventilated, and protect against extreme temperatures drivers' suits can withstand up to 1,300 degrees Fahrenheit! Ready set go...blast off?

THURSDAY   **WEEK 35**

Preview the 4 daily lessons to ensure you review or introduce skills that may be unfamiliar to students.

A Surprise Move

When Mom and dad called us together for a talk we knew something big was up. Otherwise they wouldn't hold no formal "family meeting. Even so none of us were expecting to hear the anouncement that mom made. Kids, she said in a calm voice, "your father has been offered a position up north. We'll be moving just as soon as summer vacation begins" She was met, as you can imagine by a stunned silence

Error Summary	
Capitalization	2
Language Usage	1
Punctuation:	
Comma	4
Period	2
Quotation Mark	3
Spelling	1

MONDAY   **WEEK 36**

As dad tried to make some comforting remarks my big brother Nico was the first to respond. "Dad I can't beleive you're doing this to us I finally made it on to the basketball team for next season. We're supposed to train all summer.

Dad jumped right in, saying "you know Nico I'm sure your new school will have a coach that will be happy to have a great player like you they'd be crazy not to put you on the team."

Error Summary	
Capitalization	3
Punctuation:	
Comma	5
Period	2
Quotation Mark	1
Spelling	2

TUESDAY   **WEEK 36**

Name _____

A Surprise Move

When Mom and dad called us together for a talk we knew something big was up. Otherwise they wouldn't hold no formal "family meeting. Even so none of us were expecting to hear the anouncement that mom made. Kids, she said in a calm voice, "your father has been offered a position up north. We'll be moving just as soon as summer vacation begins" She was met, as you can imagine by a stunned silence

• dialog

MONDAY   **WEEK 36**

As dad tried to make some comforting remarks my big brother Nico was the first to respond. "Dad I can't beleive you're doing this to us I finally made it on to the basketball team for next season. We're supposed to train all summer.

Dad jumped right in, saying "you know Nico I'm sure your new school will have a coach that will be happy to have a great player like you they'd be crazy not to put you on the team."

• dialog

TUESDAY   **WEEK 36**

Lilia was the next to protest, saying, "mom, I don't want to leave. What about all my friends?"

"You'll make new friends lilia you'll see," said Mom, trying to be helpful.

"And you can keep in ~~tuch~~ touch with your close friends through e-mail," Dad added.

That was too much for me. "On what computer?" I demanded.

Error Summary

Capitalization	3
Punctuation:	
Comma	2
Period	2
Quotation Mark	5
Other	2
Spelling	1

WEDNESDAY   **WEEK 36**

Mom and dad exchanged glances, then Dad spoke. "Well, kids. Mom and I thought the least we could do to make things ~~easyer~~ easier would be to get you a new computer."

"We'll be able to have a high-speed Internet connection at the new house, too," Mom added.

Nico, Lilia, and I didn't say ~~nothing~~ anything. Sure, a new computer would help, but nothing could possibly make this move easy.

Error Summary

Capitalization	1
Language Usage	1
Punctuation:	
Comma	5
Period	1
Quotation Mark	3
Other	1
Spelling	1

THURSDAY   **WEEK 36**

EMC 2728 • Daily Paragraph Editing, Grade 5 • ©2004 by Evan-Moor Corp.

Name _____

Lilia was the next to protest, saying, mom I don't want to leave. What about all my friends

"You'll make new friends lilia you'll see, said Mom, trying to be helpful.

And you can keep in tuch with your close friends through e-mail, Dad added.

That was too much for me. "On what computer " I demanded

- dialog

WEDNESDAY   **WEEK 36**

Mom and dad exchanged glances then Dad spoke. Well kids. Mom and I thought the least we could do to make things easer would be to get you a new computer

"We'll be able to have a high-speed Internet connection at the new house, too, Mom added.

Nico Lilia and I didn't say nothing. Sure a new computer would help but nothing could possibly make this move easy.

- dialog
- semicolon

THURSDAY   **WEEK 36**

John Muir is best known as a naturalist and a conservationist because of the work he did to praise and preserve some of America's greatest wonders of nature. Write one or two paragraphs about Muir's early life and some of his early experiences with the outdoor world that will help the reader understand how Muir came to love nature. Begin with one of these topic sentences, or write your own:

- From an early age, John Muir loved nature.

- John Muir was a famous naturalist who helped preserve some of America's natural treasures.

Continue the account by Dolley Madison's sister of events related to America's War of 1812 against the British. Have the narrator (Dolley's sister) describe the scene Dolley encounters after returning to Washington, D.C., following the British attack in August 1814. She might write about the damage to the White House that Dolley has described to her, or she could write about how the fires affected the capital. Begin with one of these sentences, or write your own:

- Dolley was heartbroken when she returned home to her looted city.

- Dolley has written of devastating events in the capital city.

Describe what happens on the summer and winter solstices, and how it affects the way we experience the seasons in the Northern Hemisphere. Begin with one of these topic sentences, or write one of your own:

- Summer solstice occurs around June 21st and marks the beginning of summer in the Northern Hemisphere.

- The Northern Hemisphere experiences two solstices: summer and winter.

Do you think students should be able to help choose the foods served in the school cafeteria? Give at least three reasons to support your answer, and try to include examples as well.

Write a paragraph about farming today. Be sure to include information about the knowledge modern farmers need, the challenges they face, and the choices they must make. Begin with one of these topic sentences, or write your own:

- To be a successful farmer today, you need to know about much more than just growing crops.

- Which profession combines the skills of a good money manager with those of a trained scientist?

Write one or two paragraphs about "Pap" Singleton, his dreams, and the time in history when he lived. What were some of the changes that took place during his lifetime? How did he respond, and how did his leadership affect others? Begin with one of these topic sentences, or write one of your own:

- "Pap" Singleton lived through a time of major changes in the U.S.

- Benjamin Singleton had dreams that changed the lives of many.

- "Pap" Singleton faced many challenges as he struggled to make changes.

Write a letter that Kyoko might send home to her family or friends after her first two weeks in Chicago. Be sure to include a salutation and closing, the date, and some details about Kyoko's experiences with her new American "family."

What do you think happened when Capt. da Gama encountered the natives? Did he offer something in exchange for their gifts? Imagine you are Jorge, aboard Capt. da Gama's ship, the <u>São Gabriel</u>. Write a journal entry that describes this encounter. Don't forget to include a date. Start with one of these sentences, or write one of your own:

- I watched in amazement as Capt. da Gama walked fearlessly toward the group of men adorned in feathers and shells.

- I have seen Capt. da Gama do many brave things, but inviting the natives onto the <u>São Gabriel</u> took a lot of courage.

Write one or two paragraphs about beavers and what keeps them so busy. Be sure to mention physical features that make beavers unique. Begin with one of these topic sentences, or write one of your own:

- Beavers' ability to change their environment makes them unique in the animal world.

- Beavers are specially built for underwater activity.

- Do you know why beavers are so busy?

Write a paragraph or two describing an addition to your sand castle. What would you do to make a lake inside the castle walls? How about a castle bridge? Be sure to use words to help the reader follow the order of steps in your directions, such as *first*, *next*, and *last*.

What else do you think could happen in the land of Narnia? If you've already read the book, add more details to this book review. If you haven't, use your imagination to describe things that might happen in Narnia. Write a paragraph that begins with one of these topic sentences, or write one of your own:

- All the trees in Narnia hung heavy with cotton candy.

- In the winter, all the rivers in Narnia are completely frosted over with strawberry syrup.

Write a short news article that summarizes the story about Mark McGwire's new home run record. Be sure to cover the "5 W's" of a news story:

- <u>W</u>hat happened?

- <u>W</u>hen did it happen?

- <u>W</u>here did it happen?

- <u>W</u>hy did it happen?

- To <u>w</u>hom did it happen?

Write another paragraph that tells about what happens after the narrator's 13th birthday. Do friends and family buy the CDs the writer hoped for? Or, if you prefer, write about how you developed your taste in music. Did friends play music for you? Did you begin listening to the radio, or visiting record stores? Be sure to write in the first person.

Write one or two paragraphs to end this fable. Describe how Maui makes the net and how he captures the sun god when he comes to eat breakfast. Does Maui convince him to travel more slowly? Will the people have more hours of sunlight to grow their crops and do their work? Be sure to use quotation marks to set off the words spoken by characters in the story, and to make up a satisfying conclusion to this tale.

Write one or two paragraphs that tell about the discovery of the Great Salt Lake and some of the lake's special characteristics. Begin with one of these topic sentences, or write one of your own:

- Several rivers flow into the Great Salt Lake, but none flow out.

- An early explorer in the area now known as Utah thought he had found an inlet of the Pacific Ocean.

- Have you ever heard of a lake that's as salty as the ocean?

Write one or two paragraphs about colonial holidays. Begin with one of the following topic sentences, or write one of your own:

- People in colonial times celebrated many of the same holidays that we do today.

- Holidays haven't changed much since colonial times.

- In colonial times, families worked together to prepare for holiday celebrations.

FRIDAY – WEEK 16   **Journal Entries: Colonial Holidays**

Summarize the events that occurred on June 25, 1876, and describe the role played by Lt. Col. George Armstrong Custer. Be sure to give some background about the event and explain its importance in U.S. history. Begin your summary with one of these topic sentences, or write your own:

- On June 25, 1876, the U.S. Army experienced its worst defeat up to that time.

- Lt. Col. Custer made a number of mistakes that cost him and his troops their lives.

FRIDAY – WEEK 17   **Social Studies Article: The Battle at Little Big Horn**

Think about a familiar place. Write one or two paragraphs describing this place. Use descriptive words to make a picture of this scene for your reader. Describe what you can see, hear, and smell at this place. How do you feel when you are there? Use words that help your reader share the experience.

FRIDAY – WEEK 18   **Description: Golden Gate Bridge**

Write one or two paragraphs about the life of Jane Goodall. Be sure to say where she was born and grew up, something about her education, and about how she came to do the work that has made her famous. Begin with one of these topic sentences, or write your own:

- Jane Goodall's love of nature led to a career studying animal behavior.

- Jane Goodall was born in England, but her dream of studying animals took her to Africa.

Write one or two paragraphs that state a position that either supports or opposes a year-round school year. Begin with one of these topic sentences, or write one of your own:

- There are pros and cons when it comes to year-round school.

- I firmly believe that a year-round calendar is the best way to solve the problem of overcrowded schools.

- Summer vacation should be at least two months long.

Think about old photos you have seen. Maybe you've seen pictures of your family or of historical figures. Perhaps you've seen photos of familiar landscapes or cityscapes taken in the last century. Use your imagination to write a paragraph about one of these photographs as if it had been taken by Matthew Brady. Begin with one of these sentences, or write one of your own:

- My grandmother, Mary Ellis, was one of Matthew Brady's first photography subjects.

- The first photo of the Hudson River was taken by Matthew Brady in 1846.

Write a paragraph or two about how one of the concepts you are studying in science might be taught in an Ames Aerospace Encounter class. If you are studying gravity, you might describe how the Aerospace Encounter class could allow students to experience a "gravity-free" environment. What kind of clothing or gear would students have to wear? What would the room be like? Use your imagination and knowledge of science to write a description.

FRIDAY – WEEK 22   **Earth Science: Space Science Is Far-Out!**

Write a paragraph or two about an object that would attract a magnet. Be sure to describe the size of the object and the size of the magnet you would use to attract the object. Use one of these topic sentences, or write one of your own:

- There is a large object in my kitchen that has many magnets on it.

- There are many objects in my room that will attract a magnet.

FRIDAY – WEEK 23   **Physical Science: The Power of Magnets**

Write one or two paragraphs describing Antarctica. Be sure to mention some of the things that make this continent so unique. Be sure to use commas to separate any items that you mention in a list. Begin with one of these topic sentences, or write your own:

- Believe it or not, Antarctica was not always at the South Pole.

- Antarctica is characterized by extreme conditions.

- Did you know there is a desert at the South Pole?

FRIDAY – WEEK 24   **Social Studies Article: An Extreme Continent**

Write a letter to a friend. Describe your most recent vacation, or write about an imaginary trip that you would like to take. Remember to include the date, a salutation, a closing, and some interesting details in your letter.

Write a closing paragraph for this story about the science project. You might write about how Mario presented his project to the class, or about how Mr. Nielsen evaluated his work. Or you could tell about what Mario did with his tadpoles after the project ended. Try to include some words spoken by characters in the story. Don't forget to use commas, quotation marks, and capital letters with words in quotes.

Write a closing paragraph for this story. You might describe the creature's underwater habitat, what it eats, or how it got stuck under the rock. Or you could tell about another sighting of the creature. Be sure to use your imagination to describe details about the creature's appearance.

Can you imagine what it would be like to live in Dinotopia? Where do the dinosaurs sleep? How do humans and dinosaurs live in the same cities or use the same roads? In one or two paragraphs, use your imagination to describe an adventure or invention in Dinotopia. Use this topic sentence, or write one of your own:

- Dinotopia's new form of transportation, the Leavester, runs on solar energy.

Write a one- or two-paragraph news article that tells about the effects of a new tornado on Waverly. Describe how the tornado kits, warning system, and trained volunteers worked as planned to reduce damage and injuries caused by the tornado. Be sure to include a dateline and to present information clearly and in sequence.

Write one or two more questions and answers for this interview. Grenada Cleanup might ask another one of Mr. Tapan's students about what he or she does to conserve our planet's resources. Or Ms. Cleanup might visit your class, and she may ask what kinds of things the students in your class do to conserve our planet's resources.

Do you make your own breakfast? Can you prepare a special beverage, a dessert, or a snack? Write the directions for preparing a familiar dish that you may enjoy. Be sure to list the steps in order and use sequence words (*first*, *next*, *finally*, etc.) to help the reader follow your directions. Begin with one of the following sentences, or you may write one of your own:

- I'm very particular about the sandwiches for my lunch. Here's how I make them:

- I love the way my Grandma makes...

- It's easy to make (name of food). Just follow these simple directions:

Write a paragraph or two that describe Ernest Shackleton's experience at the South Pole. Begin with one of the following sentences, or write one of your own:

- Ernest Shackleton had a dream to travel to the South Pole.

- Ernest Shackleton and a crew of 27 men went on an expedition to the South Pole.

Write an informational paragraph that summarizes the latest developments in the search for life on Mars, the Red Planet. Be sure to mention how scientists gather information, the types of technology they use to gather and study data, and what they hope to learn with the latest Martian explorations. Use one of these topic sentences to begin your summary, or write one of your own:

- NASA's latest exploration of Mars is aimed at learning more about the history of water on the Red Planet.

- Recent scientific findings show that popular beliefs about life on Mars may have some truth to them.

Write a paragraph or two describing a character from a book you have read. You may describe the character's physical appearance, or you may write about the character's behavior or feelings. You might also like to give your opinion of this character, to say whether you like or admire the character, and explain the reason for your position.

Write a paragraph or two that explain the similarities between astronauts and race-car drivers. Be sure to explain how the force of gravity known as "G-force" affects them. You might also compare the protective gear they wear. Begin with one of these topic sentences, or write your own:

- You may be surprised to learn that race-car drivers and astronauts have many things in common.

- Do race-car drivers and astronauts have anything in common?

- The force of gravity affects astronauts and race-car drivers in a similar way.

Write another paragraph or two to continue this personal narrative. Use the same voice as the narrator to write about how the children in the family feel a few weeks after the move. Begin with one of these sentences, or write your own:

- A few weeks after the move, I was actually beginning to feel good about the change.

- The new computer was up and running a week after we moved into the new house.

- As it turned out, Nico joined a new basketball team just a few weeks after we moved.

Language Handbook

Basic Rules for
Writing and Editing

Contents

EMC 2728 • Daily Paragraph Editing • ©2004 by Evan-Moor Corp.

Capital Letters

A word that starts with a **capital letter** is special in some way.

Always use a **capital letter** to begin:

the first word of a sentence:	Today is the first day of school.
the first word of a quotation:	She said, "Today is the first day of school."
the salutation (greeting) and closing in a letter:	Dear Grandma, Thanks so much for the birthday gift! Love, Sherry
the names of days, months, and holidays:	The fourth Thursday in November is Thanksgiving.
people's first and last names, their initials, and their titles:	Mrs. Cruz and her son Felix were both seen by Dr. S. C. Lee. **Note:** Many titles can be abbreviated. Use these abbreviations only when you also use the person's name: **Mr.** a man **Capt.** a captain **Mrs.** a married woman **Lt.** a lieutenant **Ms.** a woman **Pres.** the president of a country **Dr.** a doctor or an organization
a word that is used as a name:	I went with Dad and Aunt Terry to visit Grandma. **Be Careful!** Do not use a capital letter at the beginning of a word when it is not used as someone's name: I went with my dad and my aunt to visit my grandma. **Hint:** If you can replace the word with a name, it needs a capital letter: I went with <u>Dad</u>. ⟶ I went with <u>Joe</u>.
the word that names yourself - **I**:	My family and **I** enjoy camping together.

the names of nationalities and languages:	Mexican, Cuban, and Nicaraguan people all speak Spanish.
the names of racial, ethnic, or cultural groups:	There were Asian, Native American, and African dancers at the festival.
the names of ships, planes, and space vehicles:	The president flew on <u>Air Force One</u> to see the <u>USS Abraham Lincoln</u>, a U.S. Navy aircraft carrier. **Note:** You must also underline the name of a ship, plane, or space vehicle: **the space shuttle** <u>Columbia</u>

to begin the names of these special places and things:

• street names:	Palm Avenue, Cypress Street, Pine Boulevard
• cities, states, and countries:	Los Angeles, California, United States of America, Paris, France
• continents:	Asia, Europe, South America
• landforms and bodies of water:	Great Plains, San Francisco Bay, Great Salt Lake
• buildings, monuments, and public places:	the White House, the Statue of Liberty, Yellowstone National Park
• historic events:	The Gold Rush began in 1849. The Civil War ended in 1865.

titles of books, stories, poems, and magazines:	The story "The Friendly Fruit Bat" appeared in <u>Ranger Rick</u> magazine and in a science book called <u>Flying Mammals</u>.
	
	Be Careful! Do not use a capital letter at the beginning of a small word in a title, such as **a**, **an**, **at**, **for**, **in**, and **the**, unless it is the first word in the title.
	
	Note: When you write a title, remember . . .
	
	Some titles are underlined:
	    Book Titles: <u>Frog and Toad</u>
	    Magazine Titles: <u>Ranger Rick</u>
	    Movie Titles: <u>Bambi</u>
	    TV Shows: <u>Sesame Street</u>
	    Newspapers: <u>The Daily News</u>
	
	Some titles go inside quotation marks:
	    Story Titles: "The Fox and the Crow"
	    Chapter Titles: "In Which Piglet Meets a Heffalump"
	    Poem Titles: "My Shadow"
	    Song Titles: "Twinkle, Twinkle, Little Star"
	    Titles of Articles: "Ship Sinks in Bay"

Punctuation Marks

Punctuation gives information that helps you understand a sentence.

End Punctuation

Every sentence must end with one of these three punctuation marks: **. ! ?**

A **period** (**.**) shows that a sentence is:

giving information:	I love to read short stories.

giving a mild command:	Choose a short story to read aloud.
	
	Note: A period is also used in:
	
	• abbreviations of months and days:
	    Jan. (January), Feb. (February), Mon. (Monday), etc.
	
	• abbreviations of measurements:
	    ft. (foot/feet), in. (inch/inches),
	    lb./lbs. (pound/pounds), oz. (ounce/ounces)
	
	• time:
	    8:00 a.m., 4:30 p.m., etc.

A **question mark** (**?**) shows that a sentence is:

asking a question:	Did you choose a story to read**?**

An **exclamation point** (**!**) shows that a sentence is:

expressing strong feelings:	Wow**!** That story is really long**!**

Comma

A **comma** (**,**) can help you know how to read things. Commas are often used in sentences. Sometimes commas are used with words or phrases.

Some commas are used to keep things separate. Use a **comma** to separate:

the name of a city from the name of a state:	El Paso**,** Texas
the name of a city from the name of a country:	London**,** England
the date from the year:	October 12**,** 2004
the salutation (greeting) from the body of a letter:	Dear Ms. Silver**,**
the closing in a letter from the signature:	Yours truly**,**
two adjectives that tell about the same noun:	Nico is a witty**,** smart boy. **Hint:** To see if you need a comma between two adjectives, use these two "tests": **1** Switch the order of the adjectives. If the sentence still makes sense, you must use a comma: **YES:** Nico is a witty, smart boy. ⟶ Nico is a smart, witty boy. **NO:** Nico has dark brown hair. ⟶ Nico has brown dark hair. **2** Put the word "and" between the two adjectives. If the sentence still makes sense, you must use a comma: **YES:** Nico is a witty, smart boy. ⟶ Nico is a witty and smart boy. **NO:** Nico has dark brown hair. ⟶ Nico has dark and brown hair.

   EMC 2728 • Daily Paragraph Editing • ©2004 by Evan-Moor Corp.

Some commas help you know where to pause when you read a sentence. Use a **comma** to show a pause:

between three or more items in a list or series:	Nico won't eat beets, spinach, or shrimp.
after or before the name of a person that someone is talking to in a sentence:	**After:** Nico, I think that you need to eat more. **Before:** I think that you need to eat more, Nico. **Both:** I think, Nico, that you need to eat more.
between the words spoken by someone and the rest of the sentence:	Mrs. Flores said, "It's time to break the piñata now!" "I know," answered Maya.
after an exclamation at the beginning of a sentence:	Boy, that's a lot of candy!
after a short introductory phrase or clause that comes before the main idea:	After all that candy, nobody was hungry for cake.
before and after a word or words that interrupt the main idea of a sentence:	The cake, however, was already out on the picnic table.
before and after a word or phrase that renames or gives more information about the noun before it:	The cake, which had thick chocolate frosting, melted in the hot sun. Mrs. Lutz, our neighbor, gave Mom the recipe.
before the connecting word in a compound sentence:	The frosting was melted, but the cake was great. **Note:** A simple sentence always includes a <u>subject</u> and a <u>verb</u>, and it expresses a complete thought. A compound sentence joins two simple sentences together, so each of the two parts of a compound sentence has its own <u>subject</u> and <u>verb</u>. The two parts of a compound sentence are joined by a comma and a conjunction. The conjunctions **and**, **but**, **for**, **nor**, **or**, **so**, and **yet** are all used to join two simple sentences into one compound sentence. In a compound sentence, always place the comma before the connecting conjunction: <u>Maya</u> <u>ate</u> candy, **but** <u>she</u> <u>was</u> too full to eat cake. <u>Nico</u> <u>ate</u> candy, **and** <u>he</u> also <u>ate</u> a piece of cake. <u>Nico</u> <u>is</u> thin, **yet** <u>he</u> <u>eats</u> lots of sweets. <u>Maya</u> <u>is</u> chubby, **so** <u>she</u> <u>watches</u> what she eats.

Semicolon

You can also use a **semicolon** (;) to join two simple sentences.

You may use a semicolon instead of a period to join two simple sentences:	The party ended at 4:00; the guests left by 4:15.
You may use a semicolon instead of a comma:	The party was lots of fun; however, the cleanup was lots of work! **Be Careful!** When you use a semicolon instead of a comma, do not use a coordinating conjunction (**and, but, for, nor, or, so, yet**): **With a comma:** Maya is responsible, so she wrote her thank-you notes right away. **With a semicolon:** Maya is responsible; therefore, she wrote her thank-you notes right away. **Note:** Authors may choose to use a semicolon instead of a period or a comma. It depends on the author's style or personal preference, or on the effect the author is trying to achieve in a particular piece of writing.

Quotation Marks

Use **quotation marks** (" "):

| before and after words that are spoken by someone: | "This was the best birthday party ever!" Maya said.

Note: Punctuation that follows the speaker's words goes inside the quotation marks:
"May I have a piñata at my birthday party?" Martin asked.
Mr. Flores replied, "You bet!"

Be Careful! When the words that tell who is speaking come before the quotation, put the comma outside the quotation marks. When the words that tell who is speaking come after the quotation, put the comma inside the quotation marks:
Before: Mrs. Flores asked, "Do you want a chocolate cake, too?"
After: "I sure do," said Martin. |

EMC 2728 • Daily Paragraph Editing • ©2004 by Evan-Moor Corp.

around words that are being discussed:	The word "piñata" is written with a special letter.
around slang or words used in an unusual way:	We all had to "chill out" after the party.

Apostrophe

An **apostrophe** (') helps show who owns something. You add an apostrophe after the name of an owner.

When there is just one owner, add an apostrophe first and then add an **S**:	cat + 's ⟶ cat's The cat**'s** dish was empty.

When there is more than one owner, add an **S** first and then add an apostrophe:	cats + ' ⟶ cats' All the cat**s'** cages at the shelter were nice and big.
	
	 Be Careful! When the name of more than one owner does not end with an **S**, add an apostrophe first and then add an **S**:
	
	 children + 's ⟶ children's
	     The children**'s** cat was in the last cage.
	
	 people + 's ⟶ people's
	     Other people**'s** pets were making lots of noise.

Use an apostrophe when you put two words together to make one word. This is called a contraction. In a contraction, the apostrophe takes the place of the missing letter or letters:	I + am = I'm do + not = don't you + are = you're does + not = doesn't he + is = he's are + not = aren't it + is = it's could + not = couldn't we + would = we'd have + not = haven't they + will = they'll would + not = wouldn't

Hyphen

Use a **hyphen** (–):

between numbers in a fraction:	One–half of the candies had walnuts, and one–quarter had almonds.
to join two words that work together to make an adjective before a noun:	It's not easy to find low–fat candy and sugar–free soda.

Plurals

A noun names a person, place, or thing. A **plural noun** names more than one person, place, or thing.

Add an **S** to make most nouns plural:	girl ⟶ girl + s ⟶ girl**s** river ⟶ river + s ⟶ river**s**
If the noun ends in **ch**, **s**, **sh**, or **x**, add **es**:	lunch ⟶ lunch + es ⟶ lunch**es** dress ⟶ dress + es ⟶ dress**es** brush ⟶ brush + es ⟶ brush**es** fox ⟶ fox + es ⟶ fox**es**
If the noun ends in **y**, change the **y** to **i** and add **es**:	fly ⟶ fli + es ⟶ fl**ies** story ⟶ stori + es ⟶ stor**ies** **Note:** If the noun ends in a vowel plus **y**, just add **S**: bay ⟶ bay + s ⟶ bay**s** key ⟶ key + s ⟶ key**s** boy ⟶ boy + s ⟶ boy**s** **Be Careful!** Some plural nouns do not have an **S** at all: child ⟶ **children** foot ⟶ **feet** man ⟶ **men** tooth ⟶ **teeth** woman ⟶ **women** goose ⟶ **geese**